BUILT
TO
LAST

MICHELLE A. JOHNSTON

ISBN-13: 978-1507633250
ISBN-10: 1507633254

Printed in the United States of America.

First Edition

CONTENTS

DEDICATION

This book is dedicated to the memory of a very powerful women, my mom, Patricia JoAnn Berry, thank you for pouring into me everything I would need to be a wife to my husband, a mother to my children, and a Kingdom Builder to the Kingdom. Love you mom.

ACKNOWLEDGEMENT

Life is filled with unpredictable, disturbing and hurtful events. There is a saying, 'if you have not gone through anything traumatic just live a little while longer and you will". The sheer fiber of this book is individual writings that were a desperate attempt to survive my own hurtful "life events". It was never intended for eyes to ever see let alone to be formulated into a book.

It was not until the fog of shock lifted, and I began to read all that I had written in a twenty-nine day period that I knew something supernatural had happened. There were so many that supported me during the time of fleshing out this newly birthed work. My husband, Ronald Jacob Johnston Jr, was extremely instrumental in allowing me to go on this journey and supporting me through this very emotional process. He was patient, kind and understanding for the many months it took to complete this work.

My sisters, they know who they are, held me down and would not let me quit. I am forever indebted to you for continually pushing me forward and truth be told carrying me when I could not take another step.

A great inspiration was from my mentor, the late Dr. Myles Monroe who died a tragic death at the completion of this project. Your teachings and writing are intricately woven in this book and I am so thankful you died empty, pouring out to all of us that were willing to listen.

Last but definitely not least my Pastors, Pastors John and Isha Edmondson, who so kindly wrote my foreword. They would teach me week in and week out who I am and would not allow me to succumb to my feelings and emotions but press foreword to the mark of the high calling!

FOREWORD

We are hedged in (pressed) on every side [troubled and oppressed in every way], but not cramped or crushed; we suffer embarrassments and are perplexed and unable to find a way out, but not driven to despair;

We are pursued (persecuted and hard driven), but not deserted [to stand alone]; we are struck down to the ground, but never struck out and destroyed;

Always carrying about in the body the liability and exposure to the same putting to death that the Lord Jesus suffered, so that the [resurrection] life of Jesus also may be shown forth by and in our bodies.

For we who live are constantly [experiencing] being handed over to death for Jesus' sake, that the [resurrection] life of Jesus also may be evidenced through our flesh which is liable to death. **- 2 Corinthians 4:8-11 (AMP)**

We are privileged and honored to write the forward to a piece of literature that with integrity represents the power of God responding to a person's faith and bringing them through a very trying tragic time.

As her Pastors, we have witnessed first hand Michelle stand by faith when everything in her was crying out to quit as her life was being turned upside down. Those experiences have played a major part of her journey in becoming the Woman of God she has transformed into.

Faith is not some gimmick or a product of a strong mind. It is not meant to serve as some quick way to receive what we want when we want it. True biblical faith is being able to stand on God and His promises when we find ourselves in trying, sometimes very difficult life situations.

Because of her true faith in God, Michelle has been able to successfully face and over come some mountains that would have sent others running for cover to cower down and hide. To accomplish great things in the Kingdom of God that we have been purposed to achieve, sometimes requires going through things we rather not go through. Through all that Michelle has gone through, she has stayed focused on her relationship with God and His promise to never leave her nor forsake her. [Hebrews 13:5]

Michelle's life truly displays her steadfast belief in God and her submission to God's Word regardless of how one feels. Her story is a reliable guide for trusting in God to overcome when life seems to have thrown you out into the dark abyss to disappear and be no more.

To read how she has pushed and is still pushing through feelings of frustration, discouragement, fear and helplessness to still maintain dignity, strength and hope is a testament of her unwavering faith.

Genesis 50:20 says, "But as for you, ye thought evil against me; but God meant it unto good, to bring to pass, as it is this day, to save much people alive."

We see God using this book to encourage, inspire and literally save the lives of so many who need to understand, that regardless of what you have been through, you truly are "built to last."

- Pastors John & Isha Edmondson

CHAPTER 1: THE HUMAN

> *"Your creator embedded answers to the very thing that worries you, keeps you up at nights and continually makes life very difficult on the inside of you."*

Who are you really? What are you really made of? Where did you come from and where are you going? Life has a way of posing these very difficult questions to you in the most painful and troubling ways. Have you ever just felt like buckling under the pressure? Felt like you couldn't even breathe, let alone face another day? Felt like you were not equipped or prepared to handle the tough times you are facing? If so, it shows that you are human and you are living the human experience. It is not you, you are not crazy, weak or inadequate, you are human.

Humanity carries many mysteries that can make living life difficult and sometimes impossible. In order to be built to last, you need to really know what you are made of, how you were created, who created you and why. I know the next couple paragraphs can be intense but please take your time and read through some of the science jargon and background. I promise it will be a blessing to you, remember people perish due to lack of knowledge. Knowledge truly is power and the better you understand you the more powerful you will become.

If you look up "human" in Wikipedia, it will give you a long dissertation of the human by definition and origination. It attempts to capture and explain who you are in a description of a genus group called "Homo" in the family of primates. "Homo" is a very distinct species that distinguishes itself by possessing the ability to walk on two legs, possessing a large brain with well-defined and developed sections that produce a higher level of thinking, language, and problem-solving, and building culture through social interactions. Anthropologists have attempted to dissect and understand this genus group by comparing it to the only thing they can relate it to – primates – and they have diligently tried to unsuccessfully parallel the two in an attempt to better understand this thing we call humanity.

The human has proven to be an amazing, wonderfully fashioned and designed creation that is unrivaled and impossible to parallel or duplicate. Scientists have spent centuries attempting to defragment and demystify who and what we are at our very nature and core of existence. They have been rapidly and conscientiously trying to decode what they perceive as our core – our DNA – for a long time. Much to the frustration, I am sure, of the great minds of this world, the closer they get the more they realize how far they still have to go. Unfortunately, it is not for the greatest physiologist, biologist, psychologist, or any other "ologist" to unravel. The creator intricately weaved answers in the very fibers that were used to create you, and it waits anxiously, ready to be discovered by the only person that can tap and release its own truths: you. Your creator embedded the very thing that mystifies countless others on the inside of you. It is unique and specific to you and your life's journey. It cannot be replicated or duplicated it is specific to just you.

In modern day language that makes you a superhero! Batman, Spiderman, cat women, pale in comparison to who you are as a human. The marvel movies that have dominated the great movie screens have attempted to show you what is on the inside of the human. They all experience life altering, often painful, moments that seem to give them undeniable superpowers that give them an advantage over their adversaries. With great accuracy, they play out the very thing that was meant to destroy the hero, alters them from the inside out into something supernatural. The movie writers do leave out a very important point. All humans possess that power on the inside and it is not just for an elite select few; God gave it to all of his creation. Although it is vastly exaggerated on the big screen, it still is very much real in our everyday lives.

In order to comprehend how magnificent you are made, you have to think of things in the frame of the natural mind. What you see and experience every day bears witness to how God created you special and unique. For example, when you accidentally cut yourself or injure your body in any way, miraculously, there is an immediate mechanism that is triggered to begin what we have come to know as "healing." It has been well studied, and "many answers" have been found about how the body heals. The "many answers" have led to even more mysteries and questions that we as humans clamor after every day. It is mind-boggling trying to fathom how all of these great and noble foundations and organizations commit their lives and innumerable resources to finding cures for sicknesses and diseases that seem to multiply and evolve by the hour. And, when broken down to its simplest form, scientists are just trying to get the human body to do what it appears to already know how to do: heal itself. So it begs the question if we are so amazing why are so many things wrong in this world, why sickness, disease, poverty and many more human life altering circumstances.

> *"Humans possess something very powerful on the inside of themselves. The first key is recognizing and understanding that it exists. The second key is identifying there are forces that fight it everyday to keep it unrecognized and unrealized".*

Throughout time we have seen our world and the very nature of a human spiral in and out of control in a pattern that concerns people from all backgrounds, economic statuses, and ethnicities. History tracks a consistent and continual decline of the quality of life in humanity. This is baffling generation after generation as they attempt to clamor for some hope and find answers to cease the slow yet deliberate destruction of humanity. For example, just in my lifetime, sickness coupled with evolving diseases, wars, devastating weather-related catastrophes, irreversible ecological unbalances, pervasive evil, financial devastation, and moral decline have shaken this entire world to its core. If you just take a minute to study history, you realize the things our past generations contended with have evolved and taken on a different level of difficulty. For what at first glance appears to be a step forward, there is an undercurrent of destruction at the base of the very thing we define as progress, lying in wait while we relish in great accomplishment.

There seems to be a tug-of-war between what seems to be the very "core of human nature" that desires love, joy, peace, stability, and health, and what exists around us of hate, sadness, chaos, instability, and sickness. How is it that our great minds invent great technologies that excite and change an entire world, while at the same time produce an unbelievable amount of problems and degradation? The Internet is a great example in my lifetime of this great and curious question. The Internet has had the ability to interconnect people of all ages, ethnicities, economic backgrounds, and cultures. We have access to everything and everybody, starting at birth. For example, I just saw a commercial featuring a baby in a bouncer, and where there was once an arch of toys strategically chosen to produce cognitive development, there was instead a special case created to house an iPad!

New technology has changed everything! It is a huge step forward for humans, but just as we are excited about the new opportunities it produces, a whole different side to the initial equation emerges. It births the question, "Is instantaneous access to everything always good?" We begin to see something on the inside of the human evolve and take these great advances, and learn how to build bombs that annihilate and destroy simplistic events such as the Boston marathon. It advances one's ability to not only have the depraving thoughts and actions of a child abuser but now one can access the step-by-step "how-tos" to not only feed those thoughts, but also gain access to the very thing one is after, because this "great technology" does not discriminate in age. Our families no longer sit together at the table without our devices that keep us all plugged in to a steel-cold, cyber world. Technology competes with the warm and tangible social interaction that we innately not only desire, but we really need. It is understood why we as humans embrace every advancement that takes us to the next level, but we can easily recognize there is a great price we are paying for all of our growing knowledge.

Yet through all of this, there is something in our very human nature that keeps us in the game of tug-of-war. For as much as we feel the pull on the inside toward anger, hate, sadness, chaos, instability, and sickness, we are pulling on the other side of the rope for love, joy, peace, stability, and health. No matter how intellectual and complicated things become in this world, our very human nature longs and desires to return to the uncomplicated, and to function according to the Manufacturer's plan. We are fearfully and wonderfully made, and just as something as simple as a cut on the knee miraculously figures out how to heal from the inside out, we as individual humans need to learn from the simplistic example our bodies and tap into how to heal the hurt areas of our life from the inside out. This begins with addressing the second key. What are these troubling forces and what do they want from me?

THE WAR ON HUMANITY

> *"There was no one in front of me to fight; I could not even see who or what it was. I just knew I was in clear and present danger."*

Humanity has been at war since the creation of the world for one reason and one reason only: we possess something that is desired by an adversary to our very existence. From the time Lucifer rebelled in heaven and was cast down to the earth, he has hated humanity. Due to his own choice of rebelling against a God that loved him very much, the salvation plan that went into action because of his choices, is freely offered to humanity and does not include him. He absolutely hates that human beings have the choice to love God, serve Him faithfully and ultimately spend eternity with Him. The humans that Lucifer was trying to destroy can now choose to inherit eternal life and love with the God he once loved and served.

The enemy was enraged when he understood that we could enter into a tangible, intimate relationship with God through three simple steps of accepting, believing, and confessing despite his plan to separate us from God forever. All we have to do is:

- *Accept* Jesus Christ as our Lord and Savior.

- *Believe* He died on the cross for each and every one of our sins.
- *Confess* that Jesus Christ is Lord over every area of our lives, and reigns on the right hand of the Father until He comes back for those who served and loved Him faithfully.

This precious gift of salvation was given to us freely, and it simply drives the very enemy of our souls to distraction. Remember we talked in the previous section about superheroes? They will go through great difficulties in their lives that force them to tap into something on the inside that is greater than themselves. When they do access the gift it enrages the evil forces that are around them and they go after them and try to destroy them because of what is on the inside that has now come out so they can defeat their enemy. These movies depict the truth of salvation. You need salvation to tap into that indestructible power that is guaranteed to make you built to last. Once you tap into salvation the enemy goes to a higher level of trying to destroy your newly discovered power. In order to combat this new level of challenge, it is important to understand your triune make-up.

We as humans are a three-part being: we are a spirit, we possess a soul, and we live in a body. Our spirit comes from God, that He breathed in Adam's nostrils in the book of Genesis. The spirit is the part that makes us like Him, our creator and creates us in his image. It is the part that the enemy hates and goes after. You know the saying that they are trying to break your spirit? It is the area that strengthens, sustains and anchors you to all truth. This includes all the truths that this world works so hard to obtain.

The soul is our mind, will, and intellect. This is where we battle at the core and is a doorway to break and destroy our spirit. God teaches us that this part of us is easily lost while we work so hard to gain everything this world has to offer. The enemy will bombard your soul with corrupt thoughts, ideas and passions that will ultimately override the very nature of your spirit.

Finally, that last part of our body is the flesh part of us. It really is the least important part. In our world it has become the focal point of everything that appears to be important. This perception and focus of the least part of you was well strategized by your very real enemy. It keeps you from diving deeper and focusing on what is really important: deep on the inside. We are going to dive even deeper on this in the next chapter.

David, the psalmist, gives us insight into God's mindset on humanity in Psalms 8:

> *What is man, that thou art mindful of him? and the son of man, that thou visitest him? For thou hast made him a little lower than the angels, and hast crowned him with glory and honour. Thou madest him to have dominion over the works of thy hands; thou hast put all things under his feet (Psalms 8:4, KJV)*

This scripture lets us in on a secret thought of the angels. The angels are majestic beings that freely worship and reside with God and the enemy we keep describing, Lucifer, at one time was one of them. He was the most beautiful angel, and was in charge of all the music in heaven. When he breathed, praise and worship in music exuded from him. However, the angels were confused about God's new creation. These free-will beings could make choices, and had power and dominion over all things. They seemed to be created just a little lower than God, and in His image. When Lucifer, the beautiful angel, rebelled, he hated the very existence of this creation, and has been after them even until today.

In order to understand the war on humanity, it is important to understand the one that is at war against you. God admonishes us to know the enemy's devices so that we are always prepared to deal with the onslaught and attacks. Let's be clear: your great adversary means no good thing toward you. As a matter of fact, the Word teaches us that he walks to and fro seeking whomever he may devour. In other words, he is always looking for someone he can cause havoc to, in their life, and leave discouraged, destitute, and without hope. His mission statement is to steal, kill, and destroy. He desires to steal your peace, kill your hopes and dreams, and ultimately destroy your opportunity for eternal life.

He goes after you and all of humanity with guns blazing because of the potential that lies on the inside of you. Maybe you are reading this book and you do not know anything about salvation or Jesus; you picked it up because there are all types of havoc and things going on in your life, and you just want to survive. It is important to understand that those things are not just happening randomly. There is a very real enemy after you, and he does not discriminate about whether you believe in him, God, or anything else. He exists for one purpose only: to destroy all of humanity.

There are some people reading this book who have gone or are going through some hellish situations. It is important to understand that enemy has specifically asked for you. The question that should come to mind is, "Why did the enemy ask for me?" The enemy has to ask permission to go after something that you do not even know exists. In the book of Jeremiah, God says, "For I know the plans I have for you...plans to prosper you and not to harm you, plans to give you hope and a future." (Jeremiah 29:11, KJV). The adversary has no desire for you to prosper, and he will do everything he can to keep you from having hope. He wants you to continue to think you just exist for your own purposes, and that there is not a greater purpose that lies deep on the inside of you.

Do you know the story of Job? The Word of God lets us in on a very private conversation between God and the enemy. The enemy went to God and asked if he could have His son, Job. We are all God's creation, and to this day he goes after humanity. God replied, "Yes, you can tempt him, but you cannot kill him." In other words, He allows the enemy to go after Job. Job immediately begins to go through such horrible circumstances that it is extremely hard to understand how he even survived. He lost all of his children, he became extremely ill, he lost his wealth, and his friend betrayed him. Does any of this sound familiar? Have great atrocities come to pass in your very own life?

I know the question that is on your mind. I wrestled through them during my own serious struggles, I have asked this question a thousand times: "Why?" Why did God allow the enemy to go after Job? Why is he allowed to go after you? Why do such bad things happen?" The answer is complex, but please keep reading. I promise that you will better understand, and through this understanding, you will be empowered to be victorious through every struggle in your life.

When we reach this point of despair and questioning in our humanity, there are two realms that are highly active in our lives: the humanistic realm and the spiritual realm.

THE HUMANISTIC REALM

> *The degree of the attack on your life is indicative of the level of strength that lies on the inside of you.*

The humanistic realm is what you tangibly feel and experience every day. When you just exist in this realm, you are quickly faced with questions like, "How this could happen to me? What have I done to deserve this?" I know that in my own personal hellish situation, I kept thinking, "God, I have served you faithfully for over twenty years. I have devoted my life to expanding the kingdom and have spent the last fifteen years supporting a growing ministry, and successfully being a part of building it from eleven members to over seven hundred."

I tried to live my life according to the Word of God, and for the things that I did not get right, would repent and ask God to make changes on the inside of me. I raised my children to love God and to know Him for themselves, not based on what their mom and dad believed, but on what they believed in their hearts. But despite this glowing resume, it appeared that in one night all the demons from the pit of hell were released into my life. I started to go through extreme marriage problems, and within a year and a half I tragically lost my mother, who was my dearest friend. Within months, my entire life had been turned upside down, and I was devastated and broken! I remember going to a friend of mine, breaking down in tears, and telling her that the enemy was trying to kill me. I was not just making an arbitrary statement. I felt in my mind and my body no different than if someone had broken into my home, tied me up, and put a gun to my head. Of course, I knew that in my natural sight that was not what was happening. But my physical body was experiencing fear, sadness, shame, and despair. I knew something had desperately gone wrong, and unlike fighting someone who had just broken into my home; there was no one in front of me to fight. I could not even see who or what it was. I just knew I was in clear and present danger. The enemy had had a meeting with God, and had requested me.

In order to successfully navigate these types of hellish attacks, you cannot stay in the humanistic realm. The Word of God teaches us to wrestle not against flesh and blood. I need you to think about that very carefully for a second, and do not speed through this point. Because we are incased in flesh – remember, we are three parts being – this realm is our comfort zone. We are highly dependent on our sense of sight, smell, taste, and touch. What is happening around us deeply affects our emotions, pride, decision-making, perceptions, and all of these will ultimately drive our actions. All of these things function, thrive, and drive the humanistic realm. The problem is that we fight on this very surface natural level, yet this is not where the fight exists. Do you remember when Jesus got on the boat with the disciples, and said to them, "Let's go to the other side of the lake"? He was very tired, so he decided to go down below deck and take a nap. While Jesus was resting below, the wind began to blow, and a terrible storm came out of nowhere. The disciples were very afraid. You can only imagine the fear that gripped them. Maybe they had already had an inkling that a storm was brewing, even prior to being asked to go to the other side. What was discussed amongst each other after Jesus made the request? Did they question whether they should have even listened to Jesus, knowing the weather forecast? As the wind began to blow and became more aggressive, did they begin to blame each other for being in this predicament? Did their minds begin to think about how they would never see their loved ones again? These are very natural human responses when faced with fear in a crisis situation.

The waves had begun to overtake the boat, and at that point they were pretty much convinced, and persuaded themselves and those around them, that they were going to die. This is just a side note and a point of caution: when operating in the humanistic realm in the midst of an attack on your life, the adversary is always looking to take down more than just you. The saying that "no man is an island" is indeed true. You have a profound effect on all of the people that surround you, whether you realize it or not. Everything you share, and everything that comes out of your mouth at the point of the concern, affects not only you but all those around you. Your anger, frustration, fear, and misguided or malicious words that seem to only last for a moment, have the power to affect all those that hear them. They can have such devastating consequences that they get passed down to the future generations coming behind you. This concept will be probed more deeply in the upcoming chapters.

The disciples eventually realized after much conversation that they had not yet notified the very author of the trip that they all were going to die. They went and woke Jesus and gave Him all the bad news, but it was as if Jesus were deaf. Unlike the disciple's hysterical reactions, Jesus calmly went up on deck, and in a steel-focused manner simply spoke to the wind and the waves, "Peace, be still," and everything calmed. The disciples had only been dealing with what they had seen and sensed in the human realm. Jesus knew if they had any chance for survival, he had to tap into something different than what the disciples so easily defaulted. We can learn so much from this moment. He used the adverse situation on the outside to tap into the spirit on the inside. He became a superhero in a matter of seconds and he quickly possessed supernatural powers that would change not only the devastating circumstances but transform all those that were around Him. He transcended from the human realm to the spiritual realm so he could deal with the place the fight really existed.

> *"The enemy realizes if he can fabricate the proper storm, and replicate the perfect whirlwind, that eventually it will drive you to such destructive actions that he will be successful at his attempts to kill, steal, and destroy you."*

When all hell breaks out in your life, it is very difficult in the humanistic realm to think clearly, assess your surroundings, and come up with a clear plan, like Jesus did. The enemy goes after every emotion, thought, and pride with a hunger and a vengeance that is unrelenting.

He realizes if he can fabricate the proper storm and replicate the perfect whirlwind, that eventually it will drive you to such destructive actions that he will be successful at his attempts to kill, steal, and destroy you. Please take note, that the words I am using are "replicate" and "fabricate." The enemy cannot create. He can copy, pervert, and rearrange, but he cannot create things that do not already exist. Only God can create something out of nothing.

This is important when discussing the human realm, because often the attacks that surface and the things that come to devastate our lives surprise us. The truth of the matter is that the adversary has no creative powers. He uses already existing things to produce problems in our everyday lives. That is so worth repeating; he uses already existing things to produce problems in your everyday life. Look around you at things that you know are out of the will of God for your life. It could be decisions you are making or maybe relationships you have entertained. In our human state, we sometimes give over to our anger, frustrations, and disappointments and we begin to speak things that the enemy can quickly latch onto and use during our moments of weakness. Do not be deceived: he knows the Word of God. He knows that life and death rest in the power of the tongue, and he will quickly use death words spoken to produce things in your life. Functioning in the human realm is a death sentence, mostly because we speak things onto our own selves. Remember the scripture that says:

For we wrestle not against flesh and blood, but against principalities, against powers, against the rulers of the darkness of this world, against spiritual wickedness in high places. (Ephesians 6:12, KJV)

This lets us know that in this realm we are going to wrestle. There are very real things that are going to come at us. This is the tip of the answer to why bad things happen. This scripture tells us that there are principalities, powers, and rulers of darkness in this world. This is the enemy of your soul. There was a time when we were first created that this was not the case.

The enemy existed, but man and woman were here on earth free from him and functioning the way God created them. You can read about it in the first chapters in the book of Genesis. However, due to the enemy's hatred for humanity, he went to Adam and Eve and lied to them, and convinced them to do what he had once done –to disobey God. He went after the apple of God's eye – the ones He created in His image – thinking that that would further hurt God, and destroy Adam and Eve. At the moment that the enemy convinced them to be disobedient, everything changed. The enemy's plan to destroy humanity went full steam ahead, and sin entered humanity and the earth. The generations going forward began the battle of good versus evil, and the great tug-of-war on the inside of every person began. This is how the bad things began, and why such atrocities take place in the lives of humans. God never desired for His children to suffer. He created them to live in peace, and to love and enjoy Him and everything He created. Humanity turned over ruler ship in this world to the adversary by disobeying God and gave him free reign here on the Earth.

Due to sin, God had to come up with a plan that would restore humanity back to its original state. He needed a way to gain His creation back to Himself because He loves us so much. The plan he came up with is called salvation. So, despite the fact that the enemy works hard here on this earth every day, there is a living God that is continually rolling out His plan of restoration for those that love Him, and desire to serve Him, and spend eternity with Him. We are free-will beings and the choice is ours, no different than the choice was Adam and Eve's. The enemy had to go to God for Job because Job was still a child of God. Although the adversary sets forth things in this earth under his own power and ruler ship that cause great atrocities, God has a plan that supersedes and changes the very dynamics of the enemy's plan. You are a child of God, and you are His very creation. He wants to guide you through the calamities of the enemy's plans on this earth, so you can be with Him for eternity.

My husband penned a phrase that captures this concept so well: wrestle but win! His experiences from childhood into his adulthood, coupled with God's ability to change him, comfort him, and deliver him out of all types of horrible situations, inspired him to understand that it will be a fight but he was built to last and could win. If you were to ask him, he would tell you that he could not win in the humanistic realm. You must tap into the spiritual realm in order to withstand the enemy and the many attacks he has planned on your life.

THE SPIRITUAL REALM

> *The biggest question that challenges making the switch from the human realm to the spiritual realm is, why me. It is the constant focus on feeling versus the deeper question that only the brave dig to answer and that is why not you.*

The spiritual realm gives you an advantage of truly seeing yourself as God sees you. As I was forging my way through early in building my relationship with God and dealing with some serious internal fights like loneliness, insecurity and over all feeling of just being lost, I asked God to show me how he sees me. It was life changing. I challenge you to stop right here and just ask God to reveal to you how he sees you. He began to show me through the bible, teachings and through other men and women of God how he sees me. If he did it for me he will definitely do it for you and it will change your perspective from the human to the spiritual.

He showed me the purpose and the destiny God had for my life. He brought clarity and answers to the questions that would give you great revelation as to why it is you the enemy goes after. The adversary sees something in you, and he is very afraid of the level of damage you are able to do to his plans to destroy you and those around you. However, your God left you a promise and this is the beautiful thing about choosing to be in relationship with Him. He knew and knows every problem that sin was going to produce in the lives of His children. He made sure that on this earth, while we are having these experiences, we are never alone. His promise can only become tangible as we learn to make the switch and leave the humanistic realm and live in the spiritual realm where all his promises are obtained.

The greatest tool the enemy uses to keep you from operating in the spiritual realm is temptation. For our purposes, it is not like the superficial definition of temptation, which would be equivalent to someone dangling a cupcake in front of your face, knowing you are on a diet. In its original translation, the word for temptation is "peiras-mos." It means putting a proof of, or making a proof of. If you have been in church, or around church people long enough, you have had someone tell you God will not put more on you than you can bear but with every temptation make a way of escape. I want to build some clarity around this statement. The scripture says:

There hath no temptation taken you but such as is common to man: but God is faithful, who will not suffer you to be tempted above that ye are able; but will with the temptation also make a way to escape, that ye may be able to bear it. (I Corinthians 10:13, KJV)

If you look at the scripture in context, it says there is "no tempta-tion taken you." It means temptation cannot take you. It does not take you because it has a different purpose. It is making a proof of some-thing. The question that should arise is, "What is it making a proof of?" It is making a proof of who and what is on the inside of you. In other words the adversary will come and try to get you to do certain things, he will have bad things happen to affect you in certain ways, and will plan and scheme for your destruction. However, God is saying no matter which way the temptation comes it will prove (make proof of) what is on the inside of you. If He is on the inside and you are functioning in the spiritual realm, the proof will reveal the spiritual realm and the way of escape. On the other hand if you function in the humanistic realm, and are relying on your feelings and emotions the only proof that will come out of you are feelings and emotions and you will miss the way of escape. This is the key to why we remain in situ-ations for such a long time. We just continually go through the same things over and over again and remain in the same state. We then get discouraged and feel like God is not with us and he is not hearing us when in reality we are just operating in the wrong realm and therefore not experiencing the escape.

Despite what is often told to you, situations will come and you will encounter things that are more than you can bear. You should not feel guilty, or like a weak person or weak Christian because you realize that the weight is beyond you. Our trials and suffering are not indicators that God uses to see how strong we are. To the contrary, it is to demonstrate that we have confidence in God, and that it is in his strength that our hope lays. Suffering is not a part of God's plan, or a test sent by God that carries a penalty of pass or fail, but they are places where the enemy drives us. Out of the enemy's own ignorance, suffering becomes the place where we meet God and really begin the journey of knowing who He truly is in our lives. You press pass knowing Him through the stories and experiences of others, but you know Him from the depths of your own personal experience.

How will you know God to be a healer if you don't experience His healing working power in your life? How will you know Him to be the deliverer if He has never delivered you out of anything? How will you know Him to be a provider if you are never in a position to be provided for?

Apostle Paul shares his own personal experience and how he transitions from the humanistic realm into the spiritual realm:

It certainly seemed to us as if we had gotten the death penalty. This was so that we would have confidence in God, who raises the dead, instead of ourselves. (2 Corinthians 1:9, NLT)

Despite being beaten, jailed, and experiencing many more horrific circumstances that we know of, Paul shares that it seemed like they had gotten the death penalty. It appeared to him that his life was over, and I can only imagine that that conclusion resulted in profound hopelessness. What he perceived in the natural would quickly transcend to the spiritual as he went on to state that he recognized it was all to build confidence in God. Not just any God, but a God that saved him from death-like situations and hopelessness. That his situation was beyond anything he could do himself, but nothing was too hard for his God. His physical circumstance had not changed but he elevated his mindset above and beyond what was currently happening to him.

> *"The degree of the attack on your life is indicative of the level of intimacy that you will encounter with God."*

Living in the spiritual realm allows you to see beyond what is facing you, and go to deeper levels of what God is showing you in the midst of the challenge. When I was in a really dark place one of my good friends said to me, "Michelle, I don't care what it looks like. Just remember: God is always at the center of it, and He always wins. The degree of the attack on your life is indicative of the level of intimacy that you will encounter with God."

Let's look at Peter again. Peter was walking with Jesus and became very close to him. Jesus told Peter that the adversary was asking to have him: to sift him as wheat. Why did the enemy want Peter? He wanted him because Peter had something great on the inside that the enemy was after. He had a revelation that was going to propel the New Testament church. Jesus looked at the disciples and asked a question that was bothering him: "Who does man say that I am?" Peter let all those around him answer to the best of their ability, until Jesus laid eyes on him and said, "What about you, Peter? Who do you say I am?" Without hesitation, and with great conviction, Peter said, "You are the Messiah; the Son of the living God." Jesus' next statement is the answer to why the enemy wanted Peter:

> *"Blessed are you, Simon son of Jonah, for this was not revealed to you by flesh and blood, but by my Father in heaven. And I tell you that you are Peter, and on this rock I will build my church, and the gates of Hades will not overcome it. I will give you the keys of the Kingdom of heaven; whatever you bind on earth will be bound in heaven, and whatever you lose on earth will be loosed in heaven." (Matthew 16:17-19)*

Because Peter's destiny was on the inside of him, and he knew how to see beyond what things looked like to the natural eye, it opened him up to possibilities that were not opened to the others he was around. The church was going to be built on that: it is called revelation. Revelation is the revealing or disclosing of some form of truth through communication with God. The church is not the four walls people go to every Saturday or Sunday to worship: that is a building. The church is the revelation of who God is that lies on the inside of you.

You reading and understanding this makes you no different than Peter! The enemy desires you because of the revelation God is speaking on the inside of you: the revelation of who you are, and more importantly, who you are in the Kingdom of God, and what you are going to do to change the destiny of humanity! God wants to silence the voice that instills fear and devastation in your life and which renders you immobile and incapable of doing the great things that He has for you.

Everyone's attack and journey is different. The enemy may have gotten you so inundated with this world's concerns – money, power, fame, bills, lust – that the concept of even having a purpose beyond your daily wants and needs is irrelevant. You may be fighting to overcome things from generations and generations before you have been passed down to you, and it consumes your whole life. Whatever it is, you need to know that it is all a trick of the enemy. That is why although Jesus brought bad news to Peter, letting him know the enemy was after him, he also brought good news to him, letting him know that as he continued to listen and obey the revelation that was on the inside of him, he would survive and be built to last. He even gave him insight into how he would make it through and left it in the instructional manual called the bible to help us. He said he would leave him Keys to the Kingdom.

Keys are needed to open things; they give an object the ability to gain movement, to lock things out, and to keep things safe. The Word says the keys give great power to those who have them. Jesus went on to tell Peter that whatever he binds on earth will be bound in heaven. Power is given to you here on this earth to bind things. If you study the original translation, it is "day oh": to tie or bind, or to trap and render motionless. We as humans who know who Jesus is, and who he is in our lives, have the power to tie up and render motionless demonic activity here on earth. And since heaven will be in agreement, it will be bound in heaven, too. The power is extended because then we can lose, or "loo oh": to break up or melt things on earth, and heaven will be in agreement and lose it in heaven. We then can lose the blessings, peace, love, joy, prosperity, and everything God desires for our lives.

Although bad things happen, there is power that lies beyond those bad things that turns things that are bad into things that are good. The bible tells us that all things work together for the good: for those who love God and walk according to His purpose. There is a way of escape for you. It does require your understanding of your humanity, solidifying that there is something on the inside of you that is very valuable, and acquiring the skill of moving from your humanistic realm into the spiritual realm. We talked a lot about what is on the inside of you and what will be "making a proof of" or tempted. Lets continue that thought by discussing what is on the inside of you.

CHAPTER 2: THE OLIVE

"What are you really made of?"
David the psalmist writes that God's hand shaped and formed you from the very beginning:

For you created my inmost being; you knit me together in my mother's womb. I praise you because I am fearfully and wonderfully made; your works are wonderful, I know that full well. My frame was not hidden from you when I was made in the secret place, when I was woven together in the depths of the earth. Your eyes saw my unformed body; all the days ordained for me were written in your book before one of them came to be. (Psalm 139:13-18, NIV)

Encased in your humanity, at the very core, lies a God-designed, innate ability to not only survive but to overcome all the obstacles that you face in your life. This is not just an arbitrary statement. Even as I am writing, I am facing two of the most difficult and excruciatingly painful times in my life, which have forced me into a really dark place. As I am writing now, it is coming from a place that I have never been before, and I am so devastated and broken that all I can do is listen to His still small voice and type. I really do not know what else to do accept hope that at some point, when the smoke clears, I can go back and read this and it will help me and it will help others.

Existing in this humanity, no matter who you are, how much money you have, or what ethnicity you are, you will suffer. The enemy has one desire and one desire only, and that is to destroy you; in essence, destroying your destiny. I know the statement seems repetitive, but I do not apologize for the constant reiteration. It is important to understand how much the adversary hates humanity. I believe that when this is understood, people will truly go to war against the very enemy of their soul. We go to war against those who crash planes into our buildings and kill thousands of our citizens. However, we neglect to realize that there is another enemy that is slowly killing us every day.

The psalmist David understood the struggle all too well. During his darker times he stated, "Your eyes saw my unformed body; all the days ordained for me were written in your book before one of them came to be". (Psalm 139:16, KJV) He was a man who very much struggled in his own humanity with issues such as adultery, lying, and even murder. His life exhibited great difficulties and sorrow but he was able to understand that the answers to his personal challenges were known ahead of time by His creator. One of his documented writings states that all the days ordained for him were written inside of him before they came to be. In essence, all of the sufferings, afflictions, blessings, and victories are woven in the fabric inside of us at creation. God knows everything that is going to take place and strategically fashioned you to withstand and persevere.

> *You were built to last.*

With life's challenges, there is a targeted goal to get to what was placed deep inside of you. As you read earlier in this chapter, your humanity wraps layer upon layer of things on you that hinder you from getting to the core of your peace, joy, and love that lies on the inside of you. The Word of God teaches us that in our flesh dwells no good thing. In our flesh we are encased in fear, sickness, shame, and lust: everything that is totally contrary to the God that is on the inside of us.

> *"God made sure that the very thing that was created to destroy you would produce such greatness on the inside of you, it would destroy the enemy's kingdom."*

It began in the Garden with Adam and Eve. When they sinned against God and believed the enemy's lies, their immediate reaction was fear, shame, and doubt. All of these were the beginning building blocks of what would become of this "new humanity." They never felt anything like this on their flesh: it was foreign to them and scary. It forced Adam and Eve to run and hide, in hopes that the feeling would just go away. It is no different today. Layer after layer of insecurities, tiredness, fear, and shame pile up as the enemy sets traps for you and your family in hopes that you will run and hide from the very one that can deliver you from yourself.

However, God created a plan, already knowing the fate of humanity. He masterminded not only a strategy of redeeming us back to Himself, but a counter attack to the many afflictions that come along with this new, complex life. He made sure that the very thing that was created to destroy you would produce such greatness on the inside of you that it would destroy the enemy's kingdom. It would put into motion a surefire plan that would break through the outer encasement and open up, so the treasure in earthly vessels could flow.

A parallel example would be the olive. For centuries, people have understood that inside the olive lies a great treasure: olive oil. They used olive oil for cooking, as medicine, and in religious ceremonies. It is an expensive oil that has great value and great worth. It is similar to you.

There are so many things deep on the inside of you that have such great value and great worth. The bible teaches that it is a treasure in earthen vessels, and that you really are fearfully and wonderfully made, and created on purpose, specifically designed for great purpose. God had you on his mind, and when He began to place the treasure on the inside and wrap it in human flesh, he knew there would a process to get to what was on the inside.

The olive grows on trees that first have to withstand many destructive elements that are continually coming to destroy them. People, insects, and disease have been instruments used to keep the olive from reaching maturation so that we may benefit from its treasure.

It is amazing to see the similarities between humanity and olives. People will continually be a vessel that the enemy uses to try to destroy what God has placed on the inside of you. The valuable treasure that was given to you, and you alone, every demon in hell will use tricks to try to derail, destroy, suppress, and prevent that greatness from coming out. This destruction process begins the moment you are born to imperfect parents with their own baggage and issues. The bible says we are born into sin, and it is lying there waiting for us.

There are illnesses and infestations of varying types that directly attack our bodies and physically try to hinder the treasure. It will do its best to stagnate and debilitate us so that we are unable to go through the process and fulfill the God-given destiny that was freely given. Often, we are infested with the inability to shed the years of layers on us, and it wears away at us, destroying us from the outside in, making it impossible to go through the process to extract the treasure.

The olive is an excellent example of not only the challenges but also the process humanity goes through. When the olive is under pressure and enduring through these truly destructive elements, the tree is violently shaken, so the ripe and ready olives fall to the ground. We also experience shaking in our lives during times of affliction. I am feeling it right now. Whether the shaking is caused by people, sickness, loss of loved ones, trauma, or calamity; whatever is causing us "disease," the shaking is taking place.

The olives are then gathered and begin the washing, or the cleaning process. This part of the process is where we often become stagnant, or caught in a revolving cycle. The washing and the cleaning of the outside of the olive of impurities allows for the purity of what's on the inside during the crushing process to not be tainted by all the layers of debris we collect on the outside. In other words, the washing and the cleaning is symbolic of what the Word will do for us once the shaking has begun and you are knocked to the ground. This is why you cannot stop praying, reading your word and going to church when things get difficult. The word of God needs to be even more prevalent in your life during this time because of what the Word of God will do for you.

> *The Word of God is alive and active. Sharper than any double-edged sword, it penetrates even to the dividing soul (mind, will, and intellect) and spirit (that comes from God), joints, and marrows; it judges the thoughts and attitudes of the heart. (Hebrews 4:12, AMP)*

When the olive is gathered and cleaned, it appears as if it is going to be destroyed; it appears that there is no hope because the only thing left is the crushing. Although it looks like you are headed for destruction, God wants you to reflect on his promises. The very thing that has come and seems like it is going to destroy your purpose and your destiny will be used as fuel to press out the greatness that lies dormant on the inside of you. You were built to last. No matter what it looks like, feels like, or smells like, every fiber of your being was purposed to come out on the other side better than the way you went in.

This part of the process carries a huge warning. This is where most people fail and find themselves in a continual state of disarray. The cleaning is painful and uncomfortable, and although very necessary, not many are willing to endure the time of cleaning and self-reflection. The Word of God comes to force us into facing our authentic selves. This is why the scripture shares that it is alive and painful. It penetrates the difficult things in our lives and challenges us to make incremental changes that shift our thoughts and attitudes of the heart.

The author also gives insight into what the Word of God will do in relation to us being a three-part being and how it affects the spirit, soul, and body. Lets build onto what we reviewed in the first chapter. Remember we discussed that the first part of is Spirit, this happened while the creator was creating and breathed spirit into Adam's nostrils. We were created with a soul (mind, will, and intellect) placed on the inside of us, so we have the ability to exercise a free will to love God and to think and to dominate and subdue the earth. Our spirit and our soul are encased in the third, and least, part of who we are, and that's our body. God made it from dirt, and it represents that weakest and most fragile part of who we really are. This is evident for all of us who have seen people who are dying when you watch the process of an articulate, expressive, and emotional being decline until the flesh part of them just gives up. Maybe you have attended viewings and have seen a body with the flesh lying lifeless in the casket. The person looks nothing like the one you knew: it is a dim representation of what you knew of the loved one who is now gone. That is because they have shed the least part of them and the very thing that made them who they are. Their spirit and soul has left them.

The Word comes to help us understand the great distinction of what we deal with and look at every day on the outside while we often ignore and neglect the more important part on the inside. It is easy to focus on what we see day to day because we are looking at it. It is real, tangible, and touchable. However, it is really a trick of the enemy. The very thing that we need to focus on is the thing that seems unreal. It is not tangible, and it is fleeting. It's not something we can put our hands on. It lies quietly beneath the surface and is easily influenced by everything being introduced to it from the outside. So, remember the layers we talked about? These layers are demonically introduced through outside forces (e.g., people, illness, and trauma) and we introduce them to ourselves through what we watch, listen to, eat, etc. With very little effort, the enemy has us battling and inundated with the emotion, feeling, and very real presence of the layers of weight being introduced DAILY. It compiles relentlessly twenty-four hours a day, seven days a week.

When you begin to allow the Word to work on you, it begins to separate out the soul (mind, will, and intellect) and the spirit (what comes from God).

SPIRIT - SOUL - BODY

When we hear teachings from the bible being preached, in song or the arts it makes clear what is from God and what is not from God, and we are faced immediately with what is wrong and what is right. We consciously have to choose whether to be humbled under the weight of seeing our authentic selves (via the Word), not liking what we see, and being willing to make a change. The very thing that you may have done all your life and it has always directly impacted your actions is faced with a challenge of recognizing that it was wrong. It forces you to see and acknowledge that it exists for one great purpose: to drive you to such levels of humility that you can repent, ask for forgiveness, and change it.

This is where the problem for many of us lies. Week after week, we sit underneath biblical teaching (in the washing process), but we ignore what is being brought to us in judgment of the heart and the mind, because ultimately, we do not want to change. Pride is very present, even when we do not recognize it for what it is. We cannot be washed and made clean if we do not want to change, and it is a direct hindrance to the process of bringing us through the mandatory and necessary process to getting to the treasure hidden in earthen vessels.

CeCe Winans articulated this part of the process in her song "Alabaster Box," depicting the life of Mary the Harlot who experienced the shaking in her life. Through Jesus' teachings she saw, recognized, and humbly desired change of her sinful state. Through great pain and anguish, and willingness to risk her life in order to be forgiven, she took a box of her most expensive perfume and anointed Jesus in front of all of those who claimed to believe in Him and love Him.

Allow me to break it down even further for better understanding. Jesus was the Word that became flesh and walked this earth. So, the very thing that we just talked about, which was sent to wash us clean, took on flesh and came to show us, in a tangible and realistic way, how to live our lives and receive what would become the written Word. While He was here, there were throngs of people who followed Him and listened to His teachings. There were many who appeared to be close to Him, and there were some who caught the revelation of who He really was. There were others who had an inability to get past their own "layers," and it hindered them from clearly understanding what this tangible act of love standing before them represented, and what it was trying to do in their lives.

This was not the case with Mary. The bible tells us that she pressed past all those who appeared to know and be close to Jesus. She was an outsider and a sinner who the men leered at with disdain. She had to have felt desperation in order to walk past all the men that were judging her, only holding a small expensive box of perfume in her hand. As she opened her greatest asset, and began pouring it on Jesus' head and feet, she fell on her face crying, wiping Jesus' feet with the mixture of tears and perfume with her hair.

All the while, those standing around were not even realizing what she was illustrating right before their eyes. Why could they not see it? They did not make the shift from the humanistic realm to the spiritual realm. Their own personal layers distorted the true picture of this broken woman slowly shedding the layers of shame, fear, and guilt. They could not see the Word that was flesh at that time begin to do what it came to do and separate out the soul and spirit. She became clear in her mind what was from God and what was not, and what parts of her needed to be changed.

Mary did something that no one else in that room was willing to do. She did something that many of us reading this book are not willing to do. She withstood the uncomfortable nature of the humbling process of cleansing through self-recognition. You cannot change until you are willing to face the parts of yourself that you are not proud of, and that make you feel bad. I know this is not an easy thing. Acknowledging your weaknesses and your shortcomings takes a process of self-reflection that is not easy.

> *Whatever rests on the inside will spill out and be revealed.*

Mary's experience aligns parallel with the olives that are pressed underneath a crushing weight, breaking down every element of the olive. Crushing will open the olive and release what is not seen below the skin of the olive. Whatever rests on the inside will spill out and be revealed. The wheel presses down over and over and over again, pulverizing the olive until it begins to separate out the outside, or casing, of the olive, and what is on the inside. It is only through this pressing and crushing under a certain amount of weight and for a certain period of time and temperature that what is inside of the olive casing can be extrapolated.

The men around Jesus began to murmur and complain, and talk about Mary. A part of the story that is often not discussed is the viewpoint and the experience of those who were observing Mary. Simon, the Pharisees, the disciples, and other devout men of God that supposedly knew God and His statutes, did not even realize that at that very moment, the Word that existed right in front of them – Jesus – was testing the true motives and intent of the heart.

The mere presence of this women walking into this room quickly shifted and became a mirror that only allowed them to no longer see her, but examine themselves. Mark explains, based on his observations, that there were some men in the room who were filled with indignation. Where did the indignation come from? Why did her presence bring all these feelings on the inside of others? This young woman, who was so pressed and consumed with her own issues, somehow transferred that press to those around her. All of a sudden, they too found themselves actively involved in the process.

Please – never forget that the scripture shared in Hebrews is clear that the Word is alive and active. You cannot be around the Word of God (teaching, hearing, and experiencing it) without it shaping a work on the inside of you. Unfortunately, there were some around who were filled with such pride and pure, selfish motives that when the pressure came and the crushing began, instead of a breaking and humility like Mary, the only thing that could come out was the poison that was on the inside. We are responsible for recognizing the bad parts of ourselves when they present themselves. We cannot justify it away, or ignore it as if it doesn't exist just because we do not want to deal with it. The moment they felt the indignation, they needed to ask themselves, "Why?" They needed to deal with the negative feelings between themselves and their God. The moment your bad parts are revealed, do not justify it away or ignore it as if doesn't exist. Expose it so the Word can wash it clean!

The tough question is, "What is really on the inside of you?" Not the "churchy" positive affirmations that you repeat, but truly acknowledging the areas that are not pleasing to God. I learned recently that this process is tied to your character. Character is that quality which is unchanging, stable, and dependable. You can only possess one of two types of characters: a character that reflects God or one that is opposite God. You cannot serve two masters, and that was the true dilemma in the room that day with Mary, Jesus, and the participants. Their characters were being tested. The test results are important because one's character produces something on the inside called "characteristics."

Do you really believe what you tell people, and what you teach from the pulpit? Are you one way in front of people, and then in your heart, in conversations, and even in secret, where no one is there but you and God, you are far from what you are presenting? What you share with your friends about God at church – are you sharing the same principles about God with your friends at school? Dr. Myles Monroe states "character is a self-imposed discipline in keeping with moral conviction." Character is self-imposed! That means no one, not even God, can give you character. You have to choose to possess good

Godly qualities. Characteristics are birthed out of your character. They are defined as a special quality or trait that makes a person, place, thing, or group different from others. This special quality is what drives what you present, how you act, and the decisions you make.

Mary's character produced the characteristics of shame, fear, and hopelessness, until it crushed in on her and she felt like she was broken in a million pieces. She consciously recognized and confronted the bad things about herself as she pressed her way amongst the ridicule and judgment. Mary had to push forward; she did not want to produce that same bad character. She humbled herself and realized quickly they couldn't break what was already broken. I still cannot help but wonder, "What was going through her head at the time she entered the home with all eyes on her?" Was she thinking, "Am I doing the right thing?" Did she feel this was the end of her? What if Jesus had judged her like the others? I can only imagine the urge she must have had just to turn around and run. In the natural, she appeared totally hopeless, exposed, and desperate, but underneath, something amazing was taking place.

> *"People may see you broken, but they do not understand the change and transformation you're going through on the inside."*

Even as I type, I realize, and you need to realize, that there are always people standing around, on the periphery, watching you during your process. It is easy to expect them to see and identify where you are and how you are feeling, but that is a mistake. A personal tragic example is losing a loved one or several loved ones like my family and I. While you are trying to process your loss, and make sense of the inner turmoil of hurt and pain, the whole world just continues to function. It is like an out-of-body experience as you watch people go on about their lives while you are in such a place of hurt and despair. You even want to scream to the top of your lungs, "Don't you know what has just happened?!"

Unfortunately, you cannot expect others to identify with, or relate to your current state. It does not matter how close they are supposed to be to you: they may not see or understand what you're going through. It is very dangerous to be dependent on people in times of personal crisis. God never said, "Trust and depend on man." He said, "Trust and depend on me." The ones closest to you might miss it. They may be too busy, or don't understand. If you are looking for a certain response, or have an expectation, the disappointment alone of their inaction can halt you dead in your tracks through the process. This is a divine moment in your life. This is between you and God. He may send those whose eyes He opens and allows them to see, and they will support and intercede, but it is not for everybody. People will always see you broken, but may not understand the change and transformation you're going through. Do not expect others to understand what is happening to you.

What is vitally important, though, is for you to understand what is happening to you, and humbly, and with courage, push through the pain. Just when the olive looks annihilated, a separation begins to form. The outside casing – the fleshy part of who you are – divides, and a beautiful, pure portion of you emerges from the destruction. Slowly, the very thing that was meant to destroy you, in a miraculous way, turns into something that has made you better, more effective, and much more valuable. Mary is crushed beyond recognition and lying before Jesus, hopeless. Just when everyone in that room counted her out, Jesus begins to speak and teach all that are watching that not only is she forgiven, but also her life-changing act of humility will ensure that she will never be the same. Her healing, peace, her call, her purpose, her destiny and prosperity came from going through a painful process of dying to herself. When you are being crushed beyond recognition, there is something miraculous happening deep on the inside. There is something miraculous happening to me. God knew what was going to happen to Mary. He knew what was going to happen to me, and He knows what is going to happen to you.

When God so meticulously created all of us, He placed something precious and valuable on the inside of us in anticipation of the enemy initiating his destructive plans in our lives. So, just when the process of the crushing begins, and we look as if we are being destroyed, what comes out of us literally changes the plan the enemy had to annihilate us.

What about you? What is laying in wait on the inside of you? You really are built from the inside out to last, but are you willing to go through the process to tap into what you need? Lets look at the next chapter and dive in and see what it is really on the inside of you! You are built to last.

CHAPTER 3: THE OIL

What is so powerful and what is so intimidating that the enemy would go through all he goes through to keep it from surfacing? What do I possess that he wants to derail so badly?"

The answer exists deep on the inside of you and understanding its purpose will be what propels you to push past the pain, discomfort and inconvenience it takes for it to be reached. There is a definite and specific use for what is on the inside of you and it has great value and meaning. Identifying and defining the treasure you possess is vital. The enemy wants you to devalue and never discover "the why" to your life. Imbedded deep in the mystery of your life is an explanation for the hellish situations you have experienced, or will experience.

In order to begin to understand what is on the inside of you, let's go back to the analogy of the oil. The oil that is produced through the crushing of the olive is symbolically compared to the treasure on the inside of you, both of which have been highly valued from biblical times through to today. Even today, olive oil is very costly to purchase as it contains many great properties for beauty and health. In the bible, you will find this oil being used to denote a setting apart by God, or you being chosen. When the oil was smeared on, it was symbolic of the power of God coming on your life, or more clearly defined as the "anointing."

But the anointing which ye have received of him abideth in you, and ye need not that any man teach you: but as the same anointing teacheth you of all things, and is truth, and is no lie, and even as it hath taught you, ye shall abide in him. (I John 2:27)

The oil, or the anointing, is something that we received from God that rests on the inside of us. It teaches and contains truths so that, when it is tapped into, it will open a greater level of understanding about life, and about your own personal journey. Dr. Myles Monroe teaches, "If you do not know the purpose of a thing, abuse is inevitable." If you do not know the purpose of the oil in your life, you will misuse it, or miss its very existence all together. "Anointing" is a word you often hear about in the Christian churches and is quite often mis-defined and misunderstood. In order to understand this in its entirety, let's look at what the bible says about the anointing and how it applies to us as human beings.

But we have this treasure in earthen vessels, that the excellency of the power may be of God, and not of us. (II Corinthians 4:7)

The two scriptures we just reviewed reveal very important information about you and your humanity. What lies on the inside of you, the anointing, is a treasure that holds great power. It is a divine connection that bypasses all outside influences, opinions, and judgments, and is available to teach you what you need to know, when you need it. Its teaching is not biased to other people's motives and agendas, and it is not perverted by this world's system, but it is pure and full of truths that have futuristic insight. In other words, the Word teaches us that the Lord orders the steps of a righteous man and woman of God. The treasure that is on the inside of us, we have as a tool that will carefully guide us in our already well-planned-out futures.

Proverbs 19:21 states that many are the plans that we have, but the purpose of God is the only thing that will prosper. This tells us that God has a purpose; He has a plan. Remember what I said in the earlier paragraph: if you do not know the purpose of a thing, abuse is inevitable. I think we spend a lot of time building our own plan and trying to get God to fit into our box, or idea. God's precious treasure that is on the inside of you will always propel you to truth: the truth of who you are. And it will draw you to your purpose. It is there to cover the weak areas of your life and give you strength for the call on your life. It allows God to flow in and through you in order to get His will accomplished on the earth. This is where people miss it. The anointing is not for you. It is for all those who need to be reached for the Kingdom. Crazy as it may be, the very thing that the adversary goes after is not even for you. It is for others who need to come and know the saving knowledge of Jesus Christ, become a disciple, and be edified. This is why if you are not doing anything for the Kingdom, you do not need the anointing.

> *Salvation is free, but the anointing is going to cost you!*

The anointing is very special, and it is something that God desires all of His children to possess. It is very sad to say that not everyone will experience this power in and on their lives. It is a privilege to allow God to operate in you and flow out of you in a way that impacts not only your life, but also the lives of anyone that is around you. There are so many who want it, but do not want to go through what it takes to possess it. There are many who want to be anointed, but they are not doing anything for the Kingdom that requires the anointing, and therefore do not need it. There is a story in the bible that illustrates this important dilemma:

At that time the Kingdom of heaven will be like ten virgins who took their lamps and went out to meet the bridegroom. Five of them were foolish and five were wise. The foolish ones took their lamps, but did not take any oil with them. The wise ones, however, took oil in jars along with their lamps. The bridegroom was a long time in coming, and they all became drowsy and fell asleep. At midnight, the cry rang out: "Here's the bridegroom! Come out to meet him!" Then all the virgins woke up and trimmed their lamps. The foolish ones said to the wise, "Give us some of your oil; our lamps are going out." "No," the wise ones replied, "there may not be enough for both us and you. Instead, go to those who sell oil and buy some for yourselves." But while they were on their way to buy the oil, the bridegroom arrived. The virgins who were ready went in with him to the wedding banquet. And the door was shut. Later, the others also came. "Lord, Lord," they said, "open the door for us!" But He replied, "Truly I tell you, I don't know you." Therefore keep watch, because you do not know the day or the hour (Matthew 25:1-13KJV).

There are several important lessons that lie in this parable that Jesus shared. The story depicts two types of people that were not just relevant at the time that Jesus told the parable, but are relevant now because people have the same struggle even today. There were five who were wise, and there were five who were foolish. Jesus is explaining that there were five women who were thoughtless and ill prepared, and then there were other women who were thoughtful and very prepared

Day after day, we go along "living" our lives without significant thought to the bigger picture: the Kingdom. We get so inundated with the cares of this world that it is easy to be lulled into a sense of thoughtlessness. In other words, you concern yourself only with the immediate needs of today without much thought of the impact on the Kingdom, let alone the next day. That is our culture now. We are an instantaneous, microwave society with very little discipline and stick-to-it mentality. In order to liberate and not condemn, I believe we are all guilty at times of this behavior. Our culture and our environment have been strategically fashioned to be all about consumption. We are a consuming society. Our time and resources are scarce and it is a fight everyday for those of us that love God to keep his agenda for us as paramount. This is why this lesson of the five virgins is so important to study.

The foolish virgins had everything they needed to meet the bridegroom, but because they didn't go the extra step and pay the price for the extra oil, they missed out on the very thing they were headed out to do – to meet the bridegroom; they missed out on being with Jesus. The wise virgins had chosen to pay the price to carry the extra oil. It was probably inconvenient and they probably didn't feel like carrying the extra oil with them, but they were willing to pay the price and endure the extra burden so that no matter what, they wouldn't miss Jesus.

I pray you are listening to this important lesson. There are so many of us like those foolish virgins in our churches, praising God and calling ourselves Christians, but we do not want to pick up our crosses and bear what we need to bear for the anointing to flow in our lives. Salvation is free, but the anointing is going to cost you.

Let's look at another example. Simon the Cyrene was just standing on the side of the road, watching an injustice take place on an innocent man names Jesus who was being accused and convicted to death. Simon would quickly become a living example of what we all need to do as believers. When our Lord and Savior dropped his cross that He was carrying on his way to die for each and every one of our sins, all of a sudden, Simon was approached to take and pick up the cross of Jesus. Jesus could no longer carry the weight alone. Isn't that what is happening now? Our Lord and Savior is reigning on the right hand of the Father and is not here. He is unable to carry the cross or the burden, and He is looking for the Simons of this time, this world, and this culture to take up the cross and continue on. We all have a cross that we are called to bear. We cannot sit idle, treating Christianity like it is a spectator sport. It is the exact opposite! It is a very physical, combative, and hands-on, life-changing decision that carries a responsibility.

What I love about the salvation story more than anything is that despite how things looked, despite how hopeless things appeared, and despite the report that the enemy won, it was the exact opposite. When Jesus took his last breath and uttered it was finished, he hung his head and his job on the cross was done, there were many that thought that was end of the story. Jesus too had to go through the pain, the inconvenience, the crushing. He went through it so he could show us how it should be done. Just like our current experiences, those that were watching Jesus did not know what was happening to Jesus on the inside. It was far from over. The oil, or the anointing, that was being birthed, and the very thing that appeared as defeat and destruction, was one of the greatest victories in history. He was winning the battle over death and the grave. He is an example and a point of encouragement on what is really on the inside just ready to spill out in our lives.

Is that your story? Do things just look hopeless, and does it appear as if you have lost and that you are down and out? I implore you to look in the spirit and not in the natural. The eyes can be very deceiving. In the spirit realm, you have just traveled to the very canals of hell, and although it appears you are defeated, it is the exact opposite. Your suffering will transform from defeat to victory. You will whoop-up on the devil, and you will rise again bigger and better with an anointing on your life that is undeniable, and will leave every demonic spirit assigned to you shivering in the fear that you opened your eyes!

CHAPTER 4: THE TRANSFORMATION

> *It is comfort that creates traditions, and discomfort that creates transformation. - Myles Monroe*

God uses nature in many ways to symbolically teach us about the amazing way our creator fashioned everything to have the ability to discover their purpose or its original intent. Everything transforms into something purposed. Trees start off as small, tiny seeds and then grow into tall, majestic, leafy oxygen-creators so that we can breathe. A beautiful bird begins as a yolk inside of an eggshell, and changes magically from an oozing, yellow substance into a bird, which maintains balance in our rodent and insect populations.

> *Everything transforms into something purposed.*

My favorite is the caterpillar because it holds a dual purpose: pre-transformation and post-transformation. Pre-transformation, it is hugely important to the food chain. It goes through a lot just to survive prior to reaching its ultimate destiny and purpose of carrying pollen to and from plants, fruits, vegetables, and flowers, so they can produce new seeds. Post-transformation, the caterpillar-to-butterfly transformation holds so many similarities to us that we will look at it more in depth.

The moment it hatches from its own egg, the caterpillar has the uncontrollable desire to eat. In its pursuit to feed this innate craving, it is fighting for its survival. They are the lowest on the food chain and are always in imminent danger of being eaten so that other animals can survive. Despite the many challenges day in and day out, the caterpillar continues to press forward, eating constantly, until it is plump and uncomfortable. It molts its skin several times trying to accommodate the growth it's creating as it continues to eat. Before long, it is so uncomfortable that it climbs a tree, hangs upside down, and begins to spin a cocoon of rest.

Just when you think the caterpillar is completely comfortable within the cocoon, it begins to release enzymes that digest its own tissue. Yes, you heard me; it literally begins a digestion process, getting rid of all of the surrounding tissue, melting into a soup-like substance. Can you imagine the discomfort, and the pain and agony that the caterpillar must go through as enzymes eat through its skin?

The enzymes will destroy every bit of tissue of the caterpillar except one highly-organized group of cells called imaginal disks. These disks will endure the destructive factors of this enzyme. While the enzyme is melting everything around it, the imaginal disks begin to form the new eyes, wings, abdomen, and legs of the new creature: the butterfly. Think about that for a minute. Placed on the inside of the caterpillar, pre-transformation, are special cells that were created to survive extreme adverse situations. Although it survives the outside dangers as they are crawling, eating and growing, it needs something special to endure the impending danger that comes with unavoidable transformation on the inside. The caterpillar was built to last!

This scenario is similar to us as humans. We go through many changes in our lifetime. As you have read in the previous chapters, you are born into a sin-filled world. The enemy is after you from the moment you enter the world. Just like the caterpillar, you are desired, hunted, and plagued by something that wants you so badly it will go through anything just to have you. On many occasions, you might have asked the question, "Why, God, did this have to happen to me? Why was I abused/molested/raped, or unwanted? Did I have to grow up in poverty, or with parents that worked constantly and never had time for me? Why have I never been comfortable in my own skin, or unable to identify who I am?" The enemy has always been right there, plaguing those that brought you into this world in the hopes that if he could get them, he would also get you.

Things in this world do not just happen. There are two very real plans at war with one another. These plans are God's plans for you, and the enemy's plans for you. God's plans are always pushing you forward to your destiny, just like He pushes the butterfly. He is pushing you to get through the difficulties, pain, and unbearable circumstances because He knows what it is going to produce.

Remember, discomfort creates transformation. You are changing or maybe you have already changed and did not even realize what the hellish situation you went through produced. You are different. There are some reading this book that struggle with shifts in their lives more than others. It is important to understand and embrace the fact that change is going to take place. No matter how hard that caterpillar may have fought to keep crawling and eating there was something propelling it to achieve the greatness on the inside. It could not control the drive to eat the last leaf, climb the tree and begin to wrap a cocoon around him. It was going to become a butterfly. The principal is the same for you. God placed something "special" on the inside of you that will always push you forward to the greatness and purpose on the inside of you. When your discomfort comes, no matter how hard, it creates something new on the inside of you that takes shape and grows. You were not created to stay the same: you were created to transform!

The question that you must ponder is, "How are you going to handle life's uncomfortable moments that manifest?" There is so much power in thinking about this prior to the change actually happening. Think about it this way: armed forces have boot camp to prepare new recruits ahead of time in anticipation that they are going to face some very tough conditions ahead. We know that attacks will come during our lifetimes, and we need to prepare ahead of time for them. When transitional attacks come, there are emotions, pride, or confusion attached to it that make it very difficult to think and process rationally. So, train ahead of time so you will be prepared to handle them.

You may not know what the adjustment will entail in detail, but you can make it up in your mind ahead of time that you will go through the process with boldness and courage. It is important that you become resolute now, so that when your transformation time comes you will endure the discomfort, pain and inconvenience knowing that there is something special on the inside developing into greatness.

The difficult times that come with transformation I call the "valley experience." Valleys are usually given a negative connotation. People will say, "I am in the valley of decision," or, "My life is in the valley," or, "I'm walking through the valley of death." Valleys, at first glance, seem far from the "mountaintop" experience. When you are in the valley you are leveled in a flat, parallel line, and everything is seen in a very linear fashion. There are no heights, no depths, or any angles. The level of sight that you are reduced to is limited to what is only in the line of direct sight. It produces a mentality of dependence on only what you can see with your linear line of sight.

National Geographic describes the valley this way: down in the valley, the land is depressed, scoured, and washed out by the conspiring forces of gravity, water, and ice. The scars left behind are known by their shapes, and where they lie. Some hang, others are hollow, but they all take the form of a "U" or "V," and the conspiring force leaves an impression that will last for decades.

As I am writing and reading this definition, I'm realizing that God wants us to identify in the valley. Yes, it is a horrible, hurtful place that is trying to develop and mold a lasting impression in our lives. In some situations, it hurts so badly that it leaves us catatonic and immobile. It takes every ounce of energy to just swing our legs over the side of the bed in order to handle the mandatories in our lives. While we are in the midst of all of that, and while I am experiencing all of this in the midst of typing, God wants us to see beyond what we are seeing, feeling, and experiencing. This can only be accomplished by identifying something bigger than the challenge we are facing. You must, and I must, pinpoint the mountain in the midst of the valley and view it from that higher point of view.

The mountains in the valley moments of your life can only be observed if you have trained yourself to have the correct thought patterns, no matter what is happening in your life. God took me to Jeremiah 29:11 as I begged for understanding on how to identify the mountain in the midst of the valley.

For I know the thoughts that I think toward you," saith the Lord, "thoughts of peace, and not of evil, to give you an expected end. (Jeremiah

> **"Change is a catalyst for new beginnings."**

I've read this scripture a thousand times, and it has never meant more to me than it does today. It came alive and became more than a scripture that I just happened to read when I found myself in my own personal cocoon. Every ounce of who I was, I can literally feel being melted away. Change is a catalyst for new beginnings. My life went into a tailspin the moment my mom was intubated and placed into the ICU. I am not sure if you have someone in your life who means everything to you, but that is how I felt about my mom. It's not just me, though. She had this infectious way of roping everyone around her into security and comfort, whether it was through her words or her magnificent cooking. My husband, who is not really the touchy/feely kind of guy, would find himself lulled into a world of touching faces and holding hands, and before he knew it he fell for her hook, line, and sinker. She was amazing.

She was the greatest grandmother ever and embraced life with passion and resolve, until she fell suddenly and deathly ill. I just knew she and I were going to walk out of that hospital together, arm-in-arm. I told her, every day of the twenty-nine days she was there, that we were leaving there together. We did not understand at the time that my mom had been very ill all along. Unbeknownst to us, she had had severe lung damage, and what we thought was asthma was a much more serious autoimmune disease. I remember going into the meeting with the doctors and hearing them say that my mother probably was not going to make it. In that instant, change began to eat away at my skin and my bones. I was numb from the excruciating pain of just the thought of her not existing.

Immediately, I audibly heard Jeremiah 29:11. For the first time, I got into an argument with God, in the lobby of the ICU hospital. Looking out of the window, I yelled, "I have served you faithfully, taking care of your church and your people! You cannot take my mom!" Again, I heard Jeremiah 29:11 and exclaimed back, "How are these thoughts of peace, and not evil? What good can come of this expected end?" I heard nothing else. There was no other response from God. He wanted me to know that His intentions toward me were for peace and that there was an expected end that He had for me. God had a plan and I needed to trust it despite how things appeared in that moment.

It took me a second, but as I sat quietly on the floor in the corner of that lobby I realized something. Prior to hearing God speak to me, I had felt one of the loneliest feelings I had ever experienced. When you are in the valley, going through change and transformation, it is often very lonely. When the caterpillar begins to spin its cocoon, there are no other caterpillars around, or inside with it. It is alone. There is great purpose in that time.

There are times in your life that God needs you to hear Him, and only Him. As I sat there His voice was so clear. Although I was angry at that voice and did not want to hear what it had to say, I heard it crystal clear. People come with a lot of their own perceptions and opinions that sometimes can be more misguiding than helpful. There are pivotal moments in your life that God needs you to hear His voice, and His voice only.

He wanted me to be clear and now you to be clear that in the midst of any devastating and quickly developing valley that will come to scar and mold and leave lasting impressions on our lives: He is there and speaking.

He needed to change my perception and he wants to change yours. He was letting me know that there was an "expected" end for my life. In order for there to be an expected end there had to be a continuation of my life. In essence, despite feeling like this was too much to handle and I was not going to make it through this situation. He was reassuring me that there was something afterwards. There was hope that under that unbearable weight of the loss of my mom that I would be able to go on. He precedes the statement of an expected end by letting us know that He thinks about you. He thinks about your purpose, and your life. Our God loves us so much that He cares for every ounce of our day, concerns, hurts, pains and challenges. It only makes sense that if He knows what He wants for your end, then He will provide everything you need starting from the very beginning of your life's journey. Much like the beautiful caterpillar, he created us with something special on the inside that will guarantee you will be built to last: He gave us Him.

He was not changing the circumstances; he was changing how I viewed the situation. While I was in agony and despair, He gave me a glimpse of a mountain: Hope. He wanted me to climb it, and look to the other side. Why you might be asking would I climb the mountain of hope? The answer is simply because you and I needed to see things differently. Things look very different from higher up; it's a very different perspective.

> *Your perspective will drive your perception, which will dictate your reactions.*

Perspective is a particular attitude toward, or way of, regarding something, or a point of view. Perception is defined as the organization, identification, and interpretation of sensory information in order to represent and understand the environment. If we combine these definitions with our statement, it reads this way.

Your particular attitude toward, or way of, regarding something, or a point of view, will drive your organization, identification, and interpretation of sensory information in order to represent and understand the environment – or, better yet, your valley.

That is why in the midst of your difficult times, the enemy is trying to get you to quit, go stagnant, or maybe even kill yourself. If he can give you a hopeless perspective, it will drive your perception and drastically effect your actions.

It is in our very nature to view things negatively, and it is work to identify the mountain, especially in the midst of the valley. How we view this life, and its very complex journey, is dependent on our most important transformation. It begins when we exchange the human nature with the nature of God, by accepting Jesus Christ as Lord and Savior. Much like the caterpillar, there is a dying to one's original self. When you are transforming, you often do not feel comfortable in your own skin. You know you are different. You do not have the same thoughts and you look at things very differently than you may have prior to your transitioning. Often, people around you will not understand you and tell you; you have changed. Change is not only uncomfortable for you, but it can be very hard for those who are around you. However, it is necessary and those who love you and want you to evolve will evolve with you.

Therefore if any man be in Christ, he is a new creature: old things are passed away; behold, all things become new. (2 Corinthians 5:17)

This vital transformation in the human form produces levels of discomfort and responsibility. It is vitally important to understand the message that Paul is trying to convey to those who carry the title of "Christian." When the scripture states, "Therefore if any man be in Christ," it is very important to understand. The original translation of Christ in the Greek is the word "Christo."

Christo is defined as anointed. This definition of Christ being the anointed one is the thing that concerns me the most about God's chosen people. What I mean by "chosen people" is that God chooses us way before we choose Him. He loves us beyond measure, whether we choose Him back or not. So, the scripture is describing if any man "be in anointed." In other words, if any man "be in the anointed." Two chapters back, we studied I John 2:27, which made clear that we receive the anointing, and it is on the inside of us. When we choose Him back, there is an exchanged that takes place: a transformation process. It is like when you look at a room in your house, and you decide you do not like it, or you want to expand it. You begin a renovation project that changes the room totally. It looks different, you have a different feeling when you come into the room, and overall it changes the total perspective of anyone that has visited your house before and now sees all the changes. It is the same principle.

When the "anointed" comes on the inside of you, it changes you from the inside out. No, you do not become perfect, but there is an evidential change in your life that continually progresses. This is not a moment that you should feel convicted but it is a moment that requires a level of candid self inspection. Is there an evidential change in your life from the time they chose Him, until now? Or, did they stop at belief? Many people say that they believe in God, and in his son, Jesus. The problem with just belief is that it does not automatically produce love, obedience, worship, or devotion. It is just belief. I have confidence in a lot of things, but I do not devote my life to serving and living by the principles of those things.

> *"If you do not allow the uneasiness to do the work that it is there to do, change cannot take place."*

The sad truth that is very rarely confronted and dealt with is that there are many believers and not enough Christians. Christians take it to the next step and go to the level of Christos, the anointed. Most people don't experience God at this level of change in their lives because they are not willing to go through what it takes for change to happen. Dr. Myles Monroe hit the nail on the head when he stated that comfort produces tradition, and discomfort produces transformation. We are easily lulled into a false sense of security as we do the same things day in and day out, building life traditions around ourselves, with not even a thought of the next step, or next level, that God has for our lives. Even if we are challenged by the thought of progression, we will quickly retreat to what we are comfortable with when one step produces a level of disquiet.

Discomfort is the catalyst that begins the transformation process. Just as the caterpillar had enzymes on the inside that would begin to break down the structure of its old form, you have a similar enzyme, and it is called discomfort. If you do not allow the uneasiness to do the work that it is there to do, change cannot take place. When you experience intense levels of discomfort, there is something that takes place on the inside that triggers what God placed on the inside of you, from the time you were in your mother's womb. The Word supports this when it says that it is in our weakness when God shows Himself strong. Think about the example of the caterpillar. When the caterpillar seems as though it is utterly destroyed inside of its cocoon, the very thing God placed on the inside, at its inception, bursts into action and begins to produce the true intent and "expected end" of the caterpillar.

Look at the birds of the air; they do not sow or reap or store away in barns, and yet your heavenly father feeds them. Are you not much more valuable than they? (Matthew 6:26)

If God will provide everything that is needed inside of a caterpillar to transition and fulfill His full intent and purpose, why would He not do the same for those who are His hands and feet in the earth? You are built to last! Everything that you need is embedded on the inside of you. You have to get out of the way and allow God to have His perfect work done in and around you.

I made the decision a while back that I was going to make my health and wellness a priority in my life. My children are older and more self-sufficient, and I really felt the need to shed all the weight that I had gained with each child, and to work toward a healthier lifestyle overall. While I am working out, one of the things that the instructor says to me is to lean in and feel the discomfort, and do not back out of it. Endure it. That is what yields the results. And that is what I am saying to you: stop running and backing out of all the painful things that are going on in your life. Lean into and endure it because that is what is producing Godly results in your life.

> *"Lean in and feel the discomfort. Do not back out of it. Endure it. That is what yields the results."*

CHAPTER 5: THE PARASITOIDS

I know many of you are wondering what in the world this chapter is about! There are so many hindrances to the transformation that God wants for your life. I could not narrow it down and put into words what I wanted to communicate in reference to this vast topic, until I came across this amazing description of something called parasitoids.

Parasitoids are parasitic insects that live on a single host with one goal in mind. It lives to reproduce itself on the inside of something or someone and the parasitoid larvae spend their time eating their host from the inside out. They literally suck the very life out of you in a selfish, self-serving manner until it is finished with you. The unfortunate hosts that often finds itself infected with these leaches are caterpillars!

Remember our beautifully transforming monarch butterfly in the earlier chapter. They often carry these parasitoids early in their development without their knowledge. Just as they are ready for the miracle to take place in their life, this unknown intruder bursts through killing the caterpillar and stopping it just short of reaching its transformation.

There are many reading this book who are on the verge of what God has for you. Your destiny is but one more step away and you have positioned yourself for your transformation and your miracle. For some, all of a sudden, your process is stopped in its tracks as these parasitic hosts rear their ugly heads. The devastating damage that the intruder has inflicted on you is so catastrophic that it eventually kills your drive toward your purpose. For others, the process is slower and much more subtle so it makes it difficult to recognize. You are lulled into a false sense of security that keeps you in a state of mediocrity avoiding all changes like the plague.

These parasitoids come in all types, forms, and ways and will latch on at different periods and times in your life. Let's just take a minute and look at a few things that can become these parasites in your life.

CHAPTER 6: RELATIONSHIPS

It is absolutely clear that God has called you to a free life. Just make sure that you don't use this freedom as an excuse to do whatever you want to do and destroy your freedom. Rather, use your freedom to serve one another in love; that's how freedom grows. For everything we know about God's Word is summed up in a single sentence: Love others as you love yourself. That's an act of true freedom. If you bite and ravage each other, watch out – in no time at all you will be annihilating each other, and where will your precious freedom be then? (Message Bible-Galations 5:13-15)

This passage is giving clear advice on how we should conduct ourselves and handle the various different relationships we will encounter along our journey. It is dealing with your relationship with your creator and those who are around you here on this earth. It very much reminds me of the statement that no man is an island. God created us to be social beings and as humans to need interaction with one another. This is why in the Garden, He said be fruitful and multiply so that there would be social interactions between His creations.

The first statement that is addressing us humans as free-will beings is very important. We have the freedom to decide the course of our lives and all those who we will allow to join us on our journey. The author admonishes us to not destroy our freedom by just running around doing whatever we want. A relationship takes a lot of thought and consideration and is not something that should be handled frivolously and carelessly.

There is no way you can be on this earth and not deal with people. Merriam Webster's dictionary defines a relationship as the way in which two or more people, groups, countries, etc., talk to, behave toward, and deal with each other. Our human interactions affect so many things and it is very sad to say that the author's advice has not been followed. The passage talks about how relationships serve and love one another and that grows and keeps your freedom. It also states that if you bite and ravage each other that eventually you will annihilate each other. There is something bad that happens when we do not operate in the simple principles of love and service. Think about it for a second; if this advice was followed there would be no wars, murders, or divorce. What a different world this would become. However, this is why relationships are in this chapter and can be a parasitoid that will lead to total destruction to your transformation.

This is not an easy topic to digest let alone execute. Although I have been saying and preaching for years that relationships are for a purpose, I have found myself putting people in places that they did not belong in my life and it has led to a lot of hurt, pain, and disappointment. These misguided relationships were hugely instrumental in hindering the call and purpose in my life. If relationships are not seriously evaluated, they can have detrimental effects on you and can lead to a continual cycle of repeated missteps that keep you off track. This topic is so vast; I am going to take time to deal with a few pivotal relationships that I believe we all navigate during our journey. As your reading just consider those in your circle and ask yourself are they a parasitoid?

I am a very social person by nature. I love people! I am invigorated by group discussions, one-on-one problem solving, and being around people who just like to have fun. One of my very clear and concise memories was the time in my life I decided that I was going to get serious for God and felt Him calling and pulling me to want to know more about Him and His character. Oddly enough the closer I drew to Him, the more the people that I depended on in my life began to fall away. I felt like all of my friends and even family were stripped away from me and it was an extremely lonely time.

> *If relationships are not seriously evaluated, they can have detrimental effects on you and can lead to a continual cycle of repeated missteps that keep you off track.*

In this difficult time of separation what surprised me the most was the challenges with my family. They are the ones who are always there no matter what happens. When you are placed in a position to be rejected by them, it can be hurtful and disheartening. I have a wonderful, loving family. Despite that fact, very early in my life I made some decisions that I believe were God led and directed and this did not sit well with them. It quickly placed me on the outskirts of my very close-knit family and the rejection, although never overtly intentional, hurt.

Simultaneously, the people whom I thought were my friends slowly and inexplicably began to drift away. And if that was not enough, God clearly let me know that despite my undying love for the young man in my life at that time, he was not my husband and I had to choose between him and God. I was devastated, broken, and alone. I really did not understand why this new journey I was on had to include the distancing from family and friends.

It felt like in an instant, God had systematically and methodically taken away what I thought were pivotal ties that kept me anchored in life. My whole world was turned upside down and I had no clue why. Although what I am about to say is not the purpose of this section, I feel that there is someone reading this who needs to hear this. God has a purpose for every season of life that may exist. The challenge is He does not always explain that season to you. This is where faith truly comes alive in your life because you have to trust that God is on the case and has your situation resting in His hands even when you are clueless as to what is going on around you. This is a necessary position for you. It is growing you and a huge part of your transformation.

> *Being built to last is allowing God to prune all areas of your life. When a plant is not pruned, it hinders its growth. When you are not pruned, it hinders your growth.*

It was such a sad and hurtful time for me and I really had a hard time tangibly identifying where God was in this and how choosing Him meant losing everything around me. He would constantly reassure me that this was a pivotal time in my life and that I was to focus on seeking Him and His perfect will for my life and with relationship comes great responsibility. At this point in my life, I had no idea what that even meant. Because relationships were and are such a huge part of my make-up, it seemed like torment and I found myself in this area of my life for what seemed like forever! I cried out in despair one night at church and God said, "Be still, daughter. You are being pruned." I immediately ran to my dictionary and looked up the word pruned and this is what I found.

Pruning is a horticultural word that is the practice of *targeted* removal of diseased, damaged, dead, non-productive, structurally unsound, or otherwise unwanted tissue. Unbeknownst to me, there were so many people, due to my social nature, who were non-productive in my life. They were not bad people. A good portion of them were proclaimed believers, but they were holding diseased, damaged, non-productive places in my life. There were some things that God needed to do with me and He needed my undivided attention without hindrances. A part of being built to last is allowing God to prune the unnecessary from your life. When a plant is not pruned, it hinders its growth. When you are not pruned, it hinders your growth. God is not trying to take something away from you; He is trying to get something to you.

Once I was well pruned, I began to see a change in me that showed me the process was working! During my alone time I really learned to depend on God like never before and I learned to hear his voice. This is huge. Often when you have too many voices around you it is hard to discern the voice of God in your life. God has a way of silencing all of the voices so you can receive direction from him. I was confident and concise in the direction God had for my life. It was not long before my family relationships were coming around and they saw very clearly that I was different and changed. As they embraced the change God was doing in my life, those relationships strengthened. I knew I felt stronger, more independent from people, and much more dependent on God.

One Sunday I went to the altar, knelt down, and said, "God, send me the friends I am supposed to have. Please allow me to have at least one friend." Imagine that, going to an Almighty God to ask for friends. It seemed so silly at the time and I remember thinking who goes to God for a friend? In retrospect, it was one of the single smartest things I have ever done.

God very quickly spoke to me about my sincere heart-felt prayer. In His still small voice, He said relationships are for purpose. It was very shortly after that plea to God that He brought three young ladies into my life and twenty years later, they are all my dearest of friends. When God purposes people in your life, and they mutually know and understand the purpose, they stick. Let me say it another way: God does not withhold any good thing from His children. I asked for friends and in time, when I was ready, He purposed friendship in my life.

He did not give me just a warm body or someone to talk to, but people who had my best interest at heart. They not only valued my goals and aspirations, but they added great value by being a tangible and significant part of my success. This last sentence I am going to repeat. They added great value. Every relationship around you should be adding to your life not taking away. Please pause for a moment and write down all of the people around you on one column. Than on the other column, list how they have been an asset in your life in some way. If you cannot think of anything, get to pruning!

The ones God sent were not jealous, malicious, and conniving, but we celebrated all of our wins together and mourned all of our losses. Everyone in your life does not have your best interest at heart. There are many reading this book who have people around them that are parasitoids. They are literally sucking the life out of you and quite frankly, God has been trying to prune them for years, but you will not let them go. He is trying to change your life and position you for growth, but you will not allow Him. Relationship pruning is transformation; it is change. It can be very painful, but go back and read the previous chapter. Go through it. It is pivotal to you being built to last.

Over the years, He has given me a much greater understanding of the power of those you let into your life. A powerful principle my pastor shares with the congregation weekly is who you are around is who you will become. One of my mentors, Dr. Myles Monroe, stated, "If you do not know the original intent of a thing, abuse is inevitable."

> *Human beings are complex and sheer force of free will on the inside of us sways us to make life-changing decisions every minute of the day. This is vital to understand because those around you at any minute can change and choose to do something different that redefines who you are in their life.*

Relationships have a specific and defined purpose. They have an original intent. If you cannot define that original intent, it is very easy to slip into an abusive situation that will impact greatly on your divine destiny. There is a duality to this thought process because relationships involve two people. This means that not only do you have to have the intent defined but also the other individual must be just as clear. The Word of God asks us how two can walk together unless they agree. There is purpose in the agreement and it allows the two individuals to move forward through very difficult times and situations.

Agreement acts as an anchor that holds things stable even when the difficult times come to challenge that union. What I mean by that is we as human beings have our own individual thought processes, baggage, history and other influences that make being "in" communication with another person very difficult. Human beings are complex and sheer force of free will on the inside of us sways us to life-changing decisions every minute of the day. This concept is vital to understand because those around you at any minute can change and choose to do something different that redefines who you are in their life. The re-definition of that relationship can take that union from healthy to abusive in an instant. Let me be clear; since we are all free-will beings, it can even be a divine relationship, but due to the other's decisions to do something different in an instant that relationship can become a parasitoid.

Relationships are not easy and should be approached in an active, well contemplated, and deliberate action. Most of us approach it from a very laid back, casual, and happenstance type of ideology. People should not just happen to you; you should happen to people. An idea that I would like you to consider implementing is a continual cyclical pattern of define, time, and maintenance. God spends a lot of time speaking to us about relationships and how we should conduct ourselves during this cyclical pattern and it is not predicated on the other person. In other words, you are held responsible for how you conduct yourself regardless of the behavior of those who are aligned around you.

DEFINE

Search through all of your relationships. Can you tangibly identify why they are in your life? Does the definition lead to something positive or does it lead to something negative? When discussing being built to last, who around you has a direct correlation to the quality of your life? This step should be done often. The reason this is the first step of the cyclical process is it allows you to be truly be honest with yourself about those who have influence over your life.

There are only two types of actions that people inflict on your life on a daily basis. It is the banking principle in relationships. The daily interactions that we have with the people around us amount to two types of exchanges. The two human beings involved are either making deposits or withdrawals. Healthy relationships find a steady state of agreed upon deposits and withdrawals that keep you in a steady state of equilibrium. The agreement is reached based on understanding the type and purpose of the relationship.

Remember if you do not know the intent of a thing, abuse is inevitable. The purpose and type of relationship you are in will dictate amounts of deposits and withdrawals as well. For example, if it is a mentoring relationship and you are the mentor, you may find yourself continually experiencing the withdrawal. However, how a mentor gets a return deposit is when the mentee grows, learns, and applies what is being withdrawn from the mentor. When the exchange becomes heavily one sided and there are just withdrawals and no evidence of productivity in what they are taking out, there becomes no deposits in the mentor's life. It is very easy to begin to feel used, unappreciated, and devalued. I mention this because in our quest to serve and love people, they can very easily fit into the parasitoid category. People love to come and just dump their garbage on people, so they can lighten their load, but have no desire to change. They will just come and take up all of your time and resources and have no intention of benefiting from the wisdom and counsel you offer. Your time is valuable and can be used for many productive things. This is a prime example of an unhealthy mentoring relationship.

Again, different types of relationships require different things, but there is always a balance that should take place. Another example would be if you are always only withdrawing from those around you, it builds a spirit of entitlement. If you are always looking for someone to do for you and not reciprocating in that relationship, it is out of balance. A balanced approach is vital and should be paramount in relationships. However, I again caution you that the union between people can begin one way and then due to the choices of one of the two, it can totally redefine the relationship and before abuse rears its head the relationship should be reevaluated.

When someone changes or begins to make really bad choices, it pulls on an emotional feeling of abandonment and rejection. Rejection is a strong emotion that emanates when someone changes the characterization of the companionship. There are so many people who spend their lives trying to overcome the residual and lasting effects that are produced after such disappointment. It is a feeling that I can relate to all too well. During a rough patch in my marriage, my husband came to me and, in honesty and with a sincere heart, said he did not know if he loved me and that he was not sure if he wanted to be married anymore. In an instant, I found myself in the cyclical pattern I mentioned above. After eighteen years and four children, my entire relationship was being redefined in an instant. The craziest and most intolerable thing about someone redefining your union is no matter how clear you are of the original intent of the relationship, people are free-will beings and there is nothing you can do about it. It is something that you now have to own and reconcile within yourself, understanding that you cannot change people. The only person you can change is yourself and you cannot control people – the only person you can control is you.

> *The only person that you can change is yourself and you cannot control people – the only person you can control is you.*

Armed with these powerful principles, you have to decide what you are supposed to do with the circumstances you are now facing. In my personal example, I immediately went to God. My example is complicated because this was my covenant partner until death do us part. Just because He wanted to redefine the original intent, it was not something I could just walk away from and let go. I had an obligation with my God to work it through. Every action from that moment going forward would either heal or harm the demonic challenge that was intruding in God's plan for my life. Please allow me to interject this point: divine relationships will always come under severe attack. The relationships that are tied to our purpose and our destiny, the enemy will go after with a tenacious fervor that will leave you shaken, despondent, and fearful. The adversary never wants those unions to produce the ultimate plan of God. With that said, expect the attack and make sure you are handling it with the same level of tenacity with which it is encroaching on your territory.

For me, my marriage and my family were at stake. I went after it with all guns blazing and began to go after it in the spirit through prayer, self-evaluation, repentance and love. I am pleased to say that my husband and I worked through it and have come out better and stronger, but in reality it is not always the fairy tale ending. If he had continued down the road of redefining who and what I was in his life, I would have made some tough decisions because once it was redefined from its original intent, abuse was sure to follow. If you are currently in that situation, seek God. He will give you so much wisdom and insight into your situation. He is faithful to order your steps and with every temptation, He will make proof of what is inside of you. It is what is inside of you that will make a way of escape.

TIME

Relationships take time. In order to make deposits and withdrawals in someone's life, you have to be there as an active participant. One of the most amazing things about the friends who God has given me is they have withstood the test of time. Through major life changes, growing families, and life's many ups and downs, they remained near and dear to my heart. True relationships are not bound by geographical location, economic status, or major life crisis. My friends and I lead very busy and complicated lives and we can go weeks or months without talking to each other and when we get together we pick up right where we left off the last time we saw each other.

I have thought about this often and wondered what we did that made our relationship so strong and so successful to weather so many major storms. The common denominator is time. We spent a lot of time together at the very beginning bonding and becoming anchored and rooted in the purpose and intent that brought us together. The mentality of defining who and why they are in my life sustained us for decades and still holds us close to this day.

The greatest example of relationship in its purest sense is found in the bible. John 15:15 states:

> *"I've told you these things for a purpose: that my joy might be your joy, and your joy wholly mature. This is my command: Love one another the way I loved you. This is the very best way to love. Put your life on the line for your friends. You are my friends when you do the things I command you. I'm no longer calling you servants because servants don't understand what their master is thinking and planning. No, I've named you friends because I've let you in on everything I've heard from the Father."*

The word friend in this scripture translates to the word *feelos* in the Greek. It means he who associates familiarly with one, a companion. Just by the nature of its original meaning it connotes an intimate, reciprocal, give and take way of operating. In my situation, early on as our relationship was growing and developing, we spent a lot of time communicating, sharing, and praying together. Friendships should be built on a positive, edifying foundation. If you are calling people your friends but they just drain you and are not adding anything helpful to your life, then you really need to look at the definition of a friend. You may have people you know, or maybe even associates, but only certain people get the title of friend.

There are so many who are destroyed simply because of the people they have around them. There is a reason that this is the longest chapter in the book. Who you surround yourself with and spend time with will impact greatly on your ability to be built to last.

I remember when my oldest daughter first entered sixth grade. If you know anything about middle school, it is the hardest period of time in a child's life. There are hormonal, emotional, and physical time bombs that are challenged at every turn in these years of their development. Jasmine is a beautiful and self-confident young lady who never got in trouble in school. Her first week of middle school, she made what I call an unsavory friend. The young lady she befriended had a very troubled background and even though her character was nothing like Jasmine's, my daughter latched onto her and they began to spend a lot of time together at school. Very quickly, I saw a change in my daughter's attitude, grades, and thought processes. When I was becoming very frustrated and trying to understand what was going on with her, it was confirmed that something was very wrong when Jasmine received her very first detention ever in school.

As I began to inquire and learn about this young lady whom Jasmine became entangled with, I quickly began to use it as a teaching tool. Who you are around is who you become. There is no way around it and the power of influence is strong no matter how much self-confidence you may project. An example I often use is the influence test. Stand up on a chair and have a friend stand in front of you. Grab your friend and see if you can pull them up to your level. It is a very difficult and, unless you are built like the hulk, an almost impossible thing to accomplish. Now use that same friend and tell them to try to pull you off the chair. I promise you it will be a whole lot easier for them to pull you down than for you to pull them up.

Influence is everything. Whatever is in your sphere of influence will control how you think. Once your thinking processes change, your actions will follow and it does not matter if it is good or bad. You will become a product of your environment.

MAINTENANCE

Intimacy's unresolved issues can breed contempt

Relationships are like new cars; in order for them to run smoothly, they must be maintained and taken care of regularly. They are work! Whenever you get two people, no matter how much they are alike, there are differences that exist and will surface. When I first got married, the very things that I loved about my husband turned into things that quickly got on my nerves. Intimacy's unresolved issues can breed contempt. The more time you spend with someone and the more intimate you are, more and more issues and challenges arise and they must be addressed and confronted. This is where the maintenance comes into play.

It is important to say this because there are so many misconceptions about the word confrontation. Confrontation is defined as a clashing of forces or ideas, or a face-to-face meeting. It carries a very bad connotation for the most part, but I am hoping to change how you look at this word. Disagreements can be handled in a very healthy and mature fashion that if wielded intelligently can produce a much better relationship on the other side of the dispute. I will reiterate, it takes a very mature approach that very few people have learned to master. The key to successfully navigating strife is having the ability to release your own personal feelings and emotions to embrace another's point of view. When you are angry and attached to being right, this is a very difficult thing to do. You have to be willing to abandon wanting to be right and embrace what is best to find resolution.

This is very powerful for any relationship, but where it is a must is in marriages. Adopting this type of pedagogy will help you preserve and maintain the relationships that are so important to you and that are divinely placed in your life to help you last. The topic of maintaining relationships is an under discussed and under valued process. I am willing to even go out on a limb and say that often the reason people become so hurt in dealing with others is because they are too busy to maintain their union.

> *Wayward relationships are used to snuff out a lot of the purpose that is supposed to exist on this earth.*

It grieves me personally when I see relationships within the Body of Christ get caught up with hurtful and often harmful relationships. The pure foundation of our belief system rests on the principle of relationship. God created us for relationship. When we broke our end of the union, He wanted to be back in interaction with us so much that He gave his only begotten son so that we would never be away from Him again except by our free-will choice. As believers we know better than to neglect and take for granted those who God sent to be such pivotal parts of our purpose and our destiny. It is only due to pure selfish motives, pride, and deception that we take the precious people who God brings into our lives and either ignore or misuse them. There are so many who come into the house of God and let their guards down only to find themselves in companionship with people who hurt and abuse them. It is particularly disturbing when they are in a place where they should be the safest.

If God has surrounded you with people of value, take care of them, honor and maintain those relationships, and guard them with your life. This is particularly vital for those of us who God has entrusted us in leadership positions and positions of authority. It is so easy to get caught up in your own vision, goals and responsibilities. While you are pre-occupied with Kingdom business you do not recognize the relational parasitoid that you have allowed to slip in and destroyed many people in the church from the inside out. Relationships are so important that when they are misused and violated, it is very difficult to rebound back from the hurt and pain. Unfortunately, wayward relationships are used to snuff out a lot of the purpose that is supposed to exist on this earth.

> *I believe mistakes are breeding grounds for un-tapped potential.*

I am not a sociologist and would not even begin to try to give you a seven-step program to different types of relationships. My purpose is to help you tangibly think about and identify who is around you and how they add value to you, enabling you to reach your ultimate purpose and destiny. We often make this way too complicated, so in my efforts to simplify let's use the best way to learn. Let's look at those who have gone before us and paved a way for us to learn from their experiences. I could have said learn from their mistakes. The word mistake has such a negative connotation and feeling and it often leads people to prolonged periods of condemnation. I believe mistakes are breeding grounds for untapped potential. When you look at it that way, although it may have been something you regret or wish did not happen, you embrace it and eventually appreciate the outcomes it produced to make you better and for you to better someone else's life through your experiences and testimony.

Once you have defined the relationship you must see if matches up to original intent God has for your life. If it does not, it can very easily slip into an abusive situation that will hinder God's will for your life. Abraham is an excellent example of this experience. If you read through Genesis Chapter 12 and 13, you read about a man who loved God and really wanted to fulfill the purpose that God had for his life. Abraham received clear instruction from God that he was to leave his country and family, pack up and go.

Although it is very easy to minimize this request from God, look at it from the scope of our discussion on relationships. Think about your own life and all the associations you have surrounding you. You have family, friends, co-workers, neighbors, brothers and sisters in the Body of Christ and all are different types of relationships. The Merriam Webster's dictionary defines relationships as the way in which two or more people, groups, or countries talk to, behave toward, and deal with each other. God is asking Abraham to abandon relationships that he has built for seventy-five years. Think about how much some of those people and connections meant to him. Of course there are certain relationships God would never ask you to abandon such as marriage because of the covenant that is established before him "till death do you part," so Sarah was a given, but everyone else was expendable.

There was a greater purpose that was destined in Abraham's life and caused him to have to walk away from people whom he loved, liked, or disliked, but all had one fine line that tied them all together and that line is relationship. This posed a very challenging quandary for Abraham and although there is only one verse in the bible that quickly states God's request, you can look at the dynamics in your own life and imagine what he must have gone through. I can only imagine the conversations Sarah and Abraham had dissecting each relevant personal relationship and how their leaving would positively or negatively affect that individual.

This was a very pivotal moment for Abraham and his decision at this point would shape and mold his destiny. His full obedience, half obedience, or total disobedience to what God had instructed would shape the upcoming chapters of his life book. This last sentence sent some theologians right through the roof, so let me qualify my statement so people can continue to read. I am not saying that there are many permissive wills of God. God has only one will and that is the perfect will of God for your life. However, if we are going to keep it real and be fully transparent, we are all guilty of getting instruction from God and following that instruction in a way as my girlfriend would say, "by putting five on it!" What that means is you add your own input or instruction and camouflage it as your being obedient. Unfortunately, this is what Abraham did. God said leave your county, and family, and go. He said yes I will go and then he allowed his nephew to come along. God never said bring Lot. As matter of fact, He said leave your family. However, relationships are not an easy thing just to leave. I have a feeling that there was such a strong relationship and he could not bear to break with his nephew Lot. The relationship had not been clearly defined and where something is not defined, abuse is inevitable.

Abraham bringing Lot along on his new journey at first thought appeared to him to be a good idea. It did not take long into his new adventure for him to find out why God commanded him to leave his country *and* family! We can learn some valuable lessons on why God requires us to define, and then either nurture or prune, some of our relationships.

✳ God's plan for your life is not conducive for everyone

When God sent Abraham, Abraham knew exactly what was going to be needed to maintain himself, Sarah, his livestock, and all of his possessions. At the moment God gives you direction on the next steps for your life, He has already made provision for you. God did not make provision for all of their stuff *and* Lot's stuff because Lot was not supposed to be there. Look at verse 5-7:

Lot, who was traveling with Abram, was also rich in sheep and cattle and tents. But the land couldn't support both of them; they had too many possessions.

They couldn't both live there – quarrels broke out between Abram's shepherds and Lot's shepherds. The Canaanites and Perizzites were also living on the land at the time. In other words, God has set resources assigned to fulfill the will and the plan he has for your life. Resources can be time, money, or food to name a few but anything that you may need to be successful at fulfilling the plane. One of the sayings that I live by is where God guides, He provides. He will provide everything that you need. When you choose to bring along those who are not a part of the divine plan, it slows down your journey, depletes your resources, causes strife, and introduces additional problems that you now have to face.

For example, my family and I went to Disney. I remember really pre-planning what to pack so that getting five others and myself through the airport and ultimately to our destination would not be horribly cumbersome. We even bought special bags, so each child could carry their own bag of stuff and could help carry the load. Of course, right before we left, all the organized plans went out the window when all of a sudden we had to take this and we had to take that. Before I knew it, bags were everywhere! It took forever to get the kids through the airport, my husband and I were frustrated and tired, and really we took on more things that we really did not need. If I had gone with the well thought out, organized, lean plan, instead of adding all the bags of additional burden, we would have sailed through the airport. Instead, I went through the last minute, not well thought out plan, and it took us a long time to get from point A to point B. That is what it is like when you are trying to drag along people with you into the well thought out, organized, Godly plan for your life. They are like extra baggage that slows you down from you ultimately getting to your destination.

> *The choice of your husband or wife can both propel you and enhance your journey or it can slow it down and hinder your purpose at every turn.*

Let's take a second to discuss one of the most important earthly relationships are or will be involved and how it affects will and plan of God for your life. Marriage is a covenant relationship that began all the way in the garden of Eve in the book of Genesis. It is a weighty and serious commitment that is treated in our culture with great disrespect and totally out of the will of its original intent. Often times we date and even marry people we should not be dating and definitely should not marry. For the awesome single people reading this book, that is why marriage should not be entered into lightly. The choice of your husband or wife can both propel you and enhance your journey or it can slow it down and hinder your purpose at every turn. It is only God that can select the one that complements His ultimate plan and even then they are free-will beings, so they may not always make the best choices that enhance your future.

Marriage, unlike many other relationships, you cannot just leave because it is additional baggage. God requires you to honor the covenant you made before Him and man, for better or worse, until death do you part. You need to evaluate all that is at stake, choose your mate wisely, and understand that your destiny will be drastically affected by your choices.

✱ When relationships are redefined from their original intent, God is not pleased and abuse does follow.

Let's look at what happened in Genesis 12:14-20 when Abraham redefined his relationship with Sarah.

When Abram arrived in Egypt, the Egyptians took one look and saw that his wife was stunningly beautiful. The Pharaoh's princes raved about her to the Pharaoh. She was taken to live with the Pharaoh.

16-17 Because of her, Abram got along very well: he accumulated sheep and cattle, male and female donkeys, men and women servants, and camels. But God hit Pharaoh hard because of Abram's wife Sarai; everybody in the palace got seriously sick.

18-19 Pharaoh called for Abram, "What's this that you've done to me? Why didn't you tell me that she's your wife? Why did you say, 'She's my sister' so that I'd take her as my wife? Here's your wife back — take her and get out!"

20 Pharaoh ordered his men to get Abram out of the country. They sent him and his wife and everything he owned on their way.

Again, if you do not know the original intent of a thing, abuse is inevitable. Redefining Sarah's purpose from his wife to his sister in the beginning seemed like it was easier, safer, and the smarter thing to do in the beginning. He could have just trusted God since God told him to go on this journey, but instead he leaned on his own understanding. It even seemed in the short term to produce a reward for Abraham.

However, when you read into the story, him redefining the original intent of his relationship with Sarah led to an abusive situation not only for his wife but also for all those involved. Think about it. Pharaoh did not take her into his home to have another servant. He saw that she was beautiful and desired to be with her. The written account does not go into detail, but can you imagine how Sarah must have felt. What did she have to endure at the hands of another man who was not her husband? Although Abraham was acquiring material things as a man, what was he going through knowing his wife was with another man? Whatever was going on in the palace, it angered God so greatly he struck

Pharaoh and the entire household with sickness just to get their attention.

In this real life example, God is showing you that when you become derailed from your purpose, God will go to great lengths to try to get you back on track. He loves you so much that He speaks to that deep inner voice, your conscience, that always tells you when you are going astray. God does not force His will on his children. He created us to be free-will beings, so as an act of our will we choose to listen to His voice. But even when we do not listen, He does not abandon His plan for us. He will intercede on your behalf because He loves you so much.

Those that are like Abraham and have been entrusted to lead family, friends or maybe even brothers and sisters in Christ, have a great responsibility. It is very easy to intentionally and unintentionally hurt the people God has placed in their trust by overlooking the importance of not redefining what God intended. The sad part about this chapter is that often people, the majority of the time, have good intentions and do not even realize they have stepped into exploiting another person. Often these hurtful situations and decisions that lead to abuse have long lasting repercussions. The recipient of this behavior becomes stuck and the prolonged repercussions of the leaders actions often have a detrimental effect. .

If you are a leader reading this book it is very important your actions do not produce this type of results. I highly encourage you to take a moment to self inspect the relationships and the people that God put in your care. If you know you did not do the right thing go to that person ask for forgiveness and rectify your wrong to the best of your ability. Self-inspection hurts but it is worth it because there is a day you will stand before God in reference to that relationship. It is also important to understand that often we hurt those around us due to our own insecurities, jealousy, and fears. Your own personal issues have redefined those relationships and have really hurt the people who were sent by God.

Saul and David were very good examples of this principle let's look at I Samuel 16:21.

And David came to Saul and served him. Saul became very fond of him, and he became his armor- bearer. Saul sent to Jesse, saying, Let David remain in my service, for he pleases me. And when the evil spirit from God was upon Saul, David took a lyre and played it; so Saul was refreshed and became well, and the evil spirit left him.

David was just a child, but he was anointed to be the next King of Israel. God allowed and purposed a relationship between Saul and David for many reasons. Although God was disappointed in Saul and did not like that he had disobeyed Him, he anointed David to take care of him during a very difficult time in his life. If you continue to read the additional chapters, you will see the relationship was reciprocal. What I mean by that is David was to benefit from the relationship by learning what to do and what not to do as king. Saul gave David different responsibilities and without knowing it was mentoring and teaching him how to be king. This is what God intended or He would have never allowed David to be placed in Saul's house. The problem arose when Saul allowed the purpose of that relationship to be redefined.

And Saul was very angry, for the saying displeased him; and he said, They have ascribed to David ten thousands, but to me they have ascribed only thousands. What more can he have but the kingdom? And Saul [jealously] eyed David from that day forward. (I Samuel 18:8,9)

Because he became intimidated and jealous of David, he changed the mentoring relationship into something that was never intended by God. He allowed pride and jealousy to get in the way and stopped doing what God intended for the alliance to accomplish and hurt David physically, mentally, and spiritually. This happens a lot in people's lives. There are relationships that you are supposed to build on and nurture for a dual purpose. There are things that the person God has placed in your care is supposed to gain and there are things that you as the leader or mentor are supposed benefit from as well. Instead the enemy comes in and you allow jealousy, division, and selfishness to drive your actions. Saul was jealous that the women were singing a song about David killing more men than he had killed. Instead of being proud that someone under his tutelage accomplished such a magnificent goal all to glorify God, he allowed jealousy to creep in and he turned on David. The enemy hates purposed things. It does not take long for him to come in and wreak havoc on God ordained relationships and after this happens many are irreparably damaged and, sad to say, that purpose is fulfilled in a different way than originally intended.

Is God troubling things that are going on around you because there are some relationships that have been redefined in your life? Are there people who have been purposed in your life and you allowed that purpose to go astray due to jealousy, lofty aspirations, or fear? Are there just people whom you never even considered what their purpose is in your life? I challenge you to find the real purpose behind the relationship and follow that purpose through.

CHAPTER 7: PATTERNS OF BEHAVIOR

And he passed in front of Moses, proclaiming, "The Lord, the Lord, the compassionate and gracious God, slow to anger, abounding in love and faithfulness, maintaining love to thousands, and forgiving wickedness, rebellion, and sin. Yet he does not leave the guilty unpunished; he punishes the children and their children for the sin of the fathers to the third and fourth generation." Exodus 34:6-7 (NIV)

One of the key components to becoming built to last is taken straight out of a quote from Shakespeare.

"To thine own self be true, and it must follow, as the night the day, thou canst not then be false to any man."

Knowing yourself is a powerful tool that is not often tapped into, which helps individuals to introspect and gives them a different viewpoint regarding how information is being processed. Although to some, this may seem like a very obvious observation, there are so many who go through life and never really know themselves. It is very easy to go through life making decisions, working on jobs, raising families and just dealing with the day to day of life and never take the time to find out who you really are and what drives all of those actions.

I began to mentor a young lady who came to me because she struggled significantly in relationships and she had no idea why every relationship she entered into ended horribly. We spent a lot of time together talking about her life, thoughts, and fears and we recognized a pattern in the way she handled relationships. When relationships would become too close and intimate, she would sabotage the association without her actions even being realized. We all need to realize that at the core of every action, there is something that is initiating the thought that drives that action. In other words, it is not something that just happens. On the contrary, it's very intentional.

This thought poses a few questions to be considered. How are your thoughts formed? Where are your decisions derived? Why do you do the things that you do? These are very pervasive, intent questions that dive into who you are and why you do what you do. Let's explore some of these thoughts and learn more about the pitfalls in our patterns of behavior.

> *At the core of every action, there is something that is initiating the thought that drives that action.*

GENETICS

As I get older and I look into the mirror, or maybe I am engaged in dialogue with a friend, I catch a glimpse of myself and there is a very familiar face staring back at me, my mom. I realize more and more how much she has influenced my life for good and bad in so many different ways.

Family history plays a huge part in what makes us who we are today. There are specific characteristics that lie in my mother that I can see in myself. For example, I can be very mouthy. There was a time in my life that I could use my mouth as a lethal weapon. When I got engaged, and my fiancé and I were seeking God on things we needed to work on to be a better wife or a better husband, God brought to my attention one scripture: set a guard at your mouth. For all my other very mouthy readers of this book, yes, there is a scripture that says set a guard at your mouth (Psalms 141:2-4). I couldn't believe it! The predominant teaching for most women who are preparing themselves for marriage are about submission, unconditional love, or maybe even being a good helpmate. The lesson that God wanted me to learn immediately was about my mouth!

After contemplating what God was trying to say to me, I thought about my own mother. She was always quick with words and did not have any problem using them. I asked her about her mom, grandmother, and great grandmother and apparently I came from a long line of strong, dominant, mouthy woman. God was trying to draw attention to something that up to the twenty-five years I had already lived I never really knew or understood about myself. He wanted me to really learn and understand myself at a deeper level because he knew what the plan was for my life and my mouth was going to get in the way. It was not just for my new marriage, but for the generations of women to come after me. I did not know at the time I was going to birth three daughters, but God knew. The answer to the challenge I was dealing with is found in the scripture cited in the beginning of this chapter. There are things that can be passed down through several generations. These characteristics do not discriminate. They can be good and bad things. The items that past generations in your family have struggled with are things that could possibly be the same struggle you are experiencing today.

Through the generations, we carry things down from parents to children in a repetitive and cyclical pattern. This pattern can go on forever until it comes across an individual who decides that they are no longer interested in repeating the cycle and they want something different for their lives and the lives of their children. As simple as I am making it sound, it is not easy to break generational cycles.

It is important to understand why this is so difficult. When you have a lineage of people that have done the same thing over and over again, it becomes the individual's norm. Please understand this pattern is not relegated to it being a good behavior or bad behavior. It is just a practice that is displayed before you so much, good or bad, that you relate to it in your brain and in your thought processes as this is normal. The only way you become confronted with your own personal normality is to come across something that is abnormal.

We are faced with abnormalities when we are exposed to things that are different than what we have always known. I cannot even begin to share with you the countless and innumerable conversations that I have had with individuals who sat across from me as I was addressing a bad, self-destructive behavior. As I began to share and open their eyes to a new type of behavior for them to consider, with tears in their eyes they would state, "Michelle, you just do not understand. This is all I know."

Allow me to use, for example, smoking to gain a better understanding of cyclical behavior patterns. We all know through years of research that smoking tobacco drastically affects the long-term health of an individual. Despite the well publicized studies and warnings, tobacco use is at an all time high. There were six million deaths associated with tobacco use just in 2013 and the industry is a multi-billion dollar trade. With that said, people stand in amazement how after all the research and studies the industry continues to grow and be profitable. The tobacco industry has tapped into and understands the power of generations. If they can hook just one individual on tobacco, and they have children, they have secured their survival for at least another generation.

Let me show you how this works. There is data obtained by naturalnews.com that a child whose parents both smoke is twenty-four percent likely to smoke. However, if neither parent smokes, then the probability for their children drops to twelve percent. The tobacco industry understands this pattern of behavior in generational cycles so well. In their efforts to use this data to their advantage, they began to produce marketing campaigns that were geared more toward children who were not even of legal age to purchase cigarettes. Although they were highly criticized for employing this type of marketing, the advertising geniuses knew that if they could continue to hold onto the children of smokers and go after the twelve percent of children from non-smoking homes, they have insured their viability for generations to come.

Smoking is a physical health example of how behaviors are passed down. Let me give you an example of a mental health issue that is prevalent and transpiring in families' patterns of behavior. *Low self*-esteem is a thinking disorder in which an individual views him- or herself as inadequate, unworthy, unlovable, or incompetent. It is reported through an ongoing study by Dr. Joe Rubino that eighty-five percent of the world's population struggles with self esteem related issues. Eighty-five percent! That number is staggering to me and hard for me to process. However, when you look at it through the eyes of patterns of behavior and generations, you can understand how this percentage has grown at an alarming rate. The Dove campaign for real beauty facilitated extensive research to try to find answers to the low self esteem epidemic.

They found through meticulous analyses that seven out of ten girls believe they are not good enough or do not measure up in some way including their looks, performance in school, and relationships. Thirty-eight percent of boys in middle school and high school reported using protein supplements and nearly six percent admitted to experimenting with steroids to improve self-image. If these young boys and girls are growing into adults, marrying and raising children, what thoughts, behaviors, ideas and values do you think are being passed down by the modeling parents? It does not take a rocket scientist to see why the percentage of low self-esteem is so high in America and it is being passed down from one generation to the next and gaining momentum.

> *Every behavior yields a result and produces something that can replicate over and over again for generations to come.*

NEW WINE SKINS

Every behavior yields a result and produces something in your life. If you have identified a cycle and patterns of behavior and you want to be the one who sets a new trend in your family tree, read carefully this concept called new wine skins. Whatever the conduct is that you desire to change, you have to create something new to replace the old behavior.

There was a time when people drank wine out of wine skins. Wine skins are simply animal skins that were dried out, treated so a seal would be created, and then sewn up into a container shape that could hold wine. They would use these skins every time they would make up a batch of wine to store it until they were ready for it to be consumed. What they quickly learned in their efforts to save time and resources was that when they would go to create a new batch of the wine and try to place the beverage in the old wine skins, it would burst wide open and what held the old wine could no longer hold the new wine. When the wine rested in the wineskin and began to ferment, it caused the skin to become brittle and fragile. As they tried to introduce the new unfermented wine into the bottle, the brittle skins did not have the strength or the fortitude to hold the new liquid.

Replacing patterns of behavior is just like this old time practice. You have behaved a certain way for a long period of time – maybe even your entire life. It has set and molded your thought processes, decision-making, and you actions. Whatever is on the inside of you changes and affects what is on the outside of you.

Someone once said to know better is to do better. The bible says that people perish through lack of knowledge. It is important to learn about yourself and gain knowledge about yourself, the good and the bad. As you gain this knowledge, and are willing to do the work to make change on the inside, you do not keep making the same mistakes over and over again on the outside and "perish" by continually making the same mistakes. As you learn a better way to conduct your life, the old ways and behaviors that rest on the inside of you become replaced by the new ways and new behaviors just like the new wine. But remember, we cannot place the new thing in the old skin. It will break open and be of no benefit to you.

You must first recognize the skin you are in is old and brittle. It is not functioning the way it was originally created to function. It is not your fault. You were born into sin and iniquity. The old skin and old ways cannot remain the same and contain this new thing you desire to operate on the inside. The treasure that is supposed to rest on the inside can not reside along with the things that are old, bad and fermented on the inside of you. You have to have a made up mind that you want something different for you and for the generations that are coming after you.

The skin is representative of everything that is not good about you. The bible teaches us that in it dwells no good thing. We are encased in this flesh that is purely selfish. It wants what it wants when it wants it. You know what I am talking about. Whether it is sex, money, power or food it drives the first onset of feelings, emotions and desires. As you change on the inside and begin to address the bad behaviors patterns and thought processes, you will need to discipline yourself to override the old skins powerfully persuasive ability to try to take you in the wrong direction. If you do not remember anything else in this book please remember this, *"greater is He on the inside of you than he that is in the world"*. As you allow God to change you on the inside He will through his word teach you disciplines to dominate what is on the outside of you hence creating new wine skins.

My husband and I walk through this process continually. We both come from broken families and we desired early on in our relationship that our children would never know what it was like to experience a broken home. However, we could not stop at just the desire. We had to make it up in our minds that divorce is not an option for us and that we needed to work our marriage out. It has to be a continual commitment to this decision because it is very easy to just revert back to what is the norm when you are breaking behavioral patterns.

We have to continually create a new mindset practice to replace the old mentality or pattern that you can just leave your marriage when things are not good. Please do not underestimate the difficulty of this type of change in your life. What will be a constant is a very real enemy that does not desire for you to make these types of advancements in your life. Much like the cigarette marketing gurus, the enemy wants you to maintain the same old patterns, so it will continue to flow from one generation to the next. He will always be there enticing you to revert to your old way of thinking.

> *Do not allow other people's issues derail you from the God given direction that generational implications in your life.*

As you persevere and continue on with a made up mind that you want something new for your life, slowly the enemy will get quieter and quieter as his schemes and attempts to derail this new transformation in your life are thwarted one Godly decision and thought at a time. This is how you create a new wine skin. It is one thought transformation at a time. There are times when my husband can disappoint me and be hurtful. It is at those times that I can hear past generations saying that you can make it on your own; you do not need to stay and be mistreated. I quickly have to counter those negative thoughts with positive reflections. I remind myself that I am in covenant with God in this relationship until death do us part and that I am committed to breaking the pattern of divorce and bad marriages that is prevalent in our families. I think about my children and the message that I want passed down to them that marriages can work with hard work and self sacrifice. Even when he was ready to quit and walk away, his actions did not dictate my re-actions. No matter what others are doing to you, you make a choice on how it will affect your response. Do not allow other people's issues to derail you from the God given direction that was intended for your life. New skin begins to grow with every opposing thought until it is stronger and stronger. Counter those negative thoughts and begin growing your new wine skin.

I have to give a word of caution to you here that it is important to be sure you are replacing the destructive pattern with something that is constructive when creating your new skin. It is very easy to stop one bad behavior and inadvertently just replace it with another poor action. In my example, you could go from breaking the thought pattern of leaving your spouse and just replace it with an equally poor pattern of living in an unhappy and unfulfilling marriage. All you're accomplishing is taking something bad and replacing it with something equally unacceptable.

Often we just want immediate relief from our feelings; our very nature is result/feeling oriented. Every behavior, good or bad, yields a result and it produces some feeling. Often the result yields a sense that continually encourages or discourages that action. The problem is everything that feels good is not good.

Once you give up one misguided pattern, you crave that instant gratification and it is easy to replace one bad device for another. There may be some temporary satisfaction in discarding the thoughts of leaving the marriage, but replacing it with thoughts of just existing in the marriage "for the sake of the next generation" hold its own negative generational patterns. It is important to make sure you are creating a sturdy, healthy skin that is pleasing to God.

Creating the new mindset and the new skin is necessary in order for it to contain the new results that the behavior will produce. New actions yield new results. The old action of smoking resulted in six million people dying in 2013 and will pass that nature down to those you influence and generations to come. Your new thoughts and the following actions of quitting smoking will result in a healthier body and you immediately become an example to those who are around you and for the next life generation coming under you that change is possible.

This is the new wine skin and the new wine and it can now be safely contained and fortified and ready to illustrate the new pattern of behavior.

> *Studying your weaknesses ahead of tumultuous times can prove to be a power tool that can save you from yourself.*

The biggest challenge to acknowledging the patterns of behavior in your life is getting past you. People do not like to hear bad things about themselves and to be totally transparent. I know that my heart palpitates when I begin to hear bad things about myself and it is a very uncomfortable experience. Learning your strengths and your weaknesses can be a tough pill to swallow. However, with knowledge, affirming or disappointing, comes great power. Studying your weaknesses ahead of tumultuous times can prove to be a power tool that can save you from yourself.

Your greatest enemy often lies "en - me." It is right on the inside of you. Everyone has weaknesses and there are no perfect people. Contrary to popular belief, learning about your weaknesses actually makes you so much stronger!

There is a very interesting misunderstanding that comes with the topic of finding out about your strengths and weaknesses that a majority of people do not understand. The most powerful way to gain this information is not by surveying yourself. I know that may sound like a rudimentary statement, but a vast majority of people are very uncomfortable asking others to evaluate them. You need the boldness and the courage to survey those around you. I am taking time with this topic because it is vital for you to understand that your weakness is not your weakness. It is your failure to identify and then deal with that weakness that is your true frailty.

Do not be embarrassed, afraid, or intimidated by the things that are not all together in your life. There are many of you for whom negative behavior is so much your normality, you do not even realize it is a weakness. We all have shortcomings and things that need to be improved. It takes boldness and courage to learn about yourself and face weaknesses in your life. If you are willing to go through this difficult process, it is life changing and can only enhance and grow you by leaps and bounds!

> *Your weakness is not your weakness. It is your failure to identify and then deal with that weakness that is your true frailty.*

AUTHENTICATING

I like to call the process authenticating. Authentic means something that is not copied or false. Our society lends to a lot of copied and false things and unfortunately has led people to live very inauthentic lifestyles. If you just take the beauty industry as one tangible example, you find a very clear message being sent to men, women and children across all ethnic and socioeconomic status groups. They have cornered the market and attempt to define beauty by their set of standards and values. The problem is those standards and values are not real. They are computer generated, airbrushed, and fabricated into unobtainable images. It was actually a cleverly derived plan from some marketing geniuses to keep a person spending money to try to obtain something that is really unattainable and inauthentic.

Who are you really? What are your true likes and dislikes? We live our lives in ways that we think we should appear a certain way or act in a particular manner that somehow translates to ourselves and to others that we are good and acceptable. It is a huge trick of the enemy to keep us from substantiating the real you. You cannot authenticate without looking at reality! It is a safety mechanism to conform to what the world around you places in the column good and acceptable. This is what is referred to as wearing a mask.

Wearing a mask is when you assume a certain visual surface appearance hoping it looks real or genuine. On the outside, you give the illusion that you are all together, but on the inside, you have much turmoil, are unsettled, and you are so uncomfortable in the skin you have created.

The enemy plays on this inauthentic behavior. He navigates his plans through the weak areas of your life. In other words, he uses them against you. It does not even matter how strong your strengths appear or how successful on the outside things appear. While you're pretending the weaknesses do not exist, he is wreaking havoc in your life and often the lives of those closest to you. Samson in the bible was such a good example of this principle. At first glance, he appeared to have everything going for him. He was handsome, strong, and popular. Unfortunately, he had an undefined weakness in his life that manifested in his relationships. Please notice I said the weakness manifested in his relationships. There is always an underlying root issue with which the struggles in your life grow. For as independent as Samson appeared to be, there was some evidence that he struggled with knowing who he really was and believing what God had told him. There seemed to be some self esteem issues that really affected and infected his life.

Although the reality was he was a very special young man and God Himself gave him a special gift of strength and power. He decided he wanted to be like another group of people although it was not in his best interest to affiliate with them. However, he wanted to fit into the column of the normal and acceptable and began to live as they lived and do the things that they did that were not true to his true self. He quickly began to be influenced and produced a pattern of behaviors that would lead to his destruction.

It is vitally important to take Shakespeare's advice and to thine own self be true. Accept and embrace who you really are and understand that God created you in that unique way for a purpose. You do not have to fit into the normal and acceptable column; it is not where you belong. Your column is the abnormal and exceptional! Produce patterns of behavior that are true to who you are and who you want to be by your God's standards not this world's.

"I call heaven and earth as witnesses today against you, that I have set before you life and death, blessing and cursing; therefore choose life, that both you and your descendants may live" (Numbers 30:19).

You do not have to fit into the normal and acceptable column; it is not where you belong. Your column is the abnormal and exceptional!

CHAPTER 8: DECISIONS, DECISIONS, DECISIONS

> *"Well thought out choices of today are the driving force for tomorrow's well executed results, and position us well for the next day's choices; Poor, rash, and impulsive choices of today lead to many devastating ripple effects of results that can be felt for generations."*

When thinking about relationships and patterns of behavior, there is a symbiotic driver to these two topics called decisions. At the core of every relationship and behavior decisions are being freely made. It is imperative that we talk about this illusive topic of free will and the decisions that come from this very powerful position. It lies in this chapter on parasitoids because I have found after studying the patterns of people that decisions directly affect outcomes. Well thought out choices of today are the driving force for tomorrow's well executed results, and position us well for the next day's choices; Poor, rash, and impulsive choices of today lead to many devastating ripple effects of results that can be felt for generations.

How one comes to a conclusion and then acts on that summation is vitally important if you are actively going to participate in building your future and protect your greatest asset, yourself. Billions of dollars are spent researching the mind and how it processes information and how decisions are developed. It can be such a mystery that criminals who commit heinous crimes are studied for years in efforts to understand what would make a person do such a horrible thing. The question is, what makes people do bad things, think detrimental thoughts, and commit unthinkable actions? Is it due to a traumatic childhood, mental illness, or maybe even the devil himself made them execute the horrendous atrocity?

I heard someone say once that as free-will agents, if we are given the opportunity to make a decision it is more than likely to be the wrong decision. This statement disturbed me and it made me begin to study and dive into the idea of our free will and our very important right to choose our everyday actions that quickly add up to our destiny or better yet our outcomes.

OUTCOME BASED DECISION MODEL

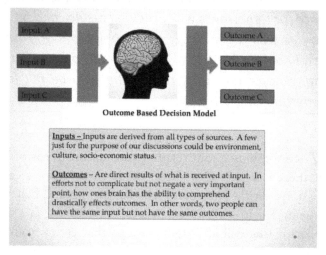

Outcome Based Decision Model

Inputs – Inputs are derived from all types of sources. A few just for the purpose of our discussions could be environment, culture, socio-economic status.

Outcomes – Are direct results of what is received at input. In efforts not to complicate but not negate a very important point, how ones brain has the ability to comprehend drastically effects outcomes. In other words, two people can have the same input but not have the same outcomes.

As a man thinketh in his heart so is he. Proverbs 23:7

It is just my natural design to look to science when trying to understand how we operate. Due to the serious nature of decisions, I believe it is important for us to explore how we are created to understand how we make our choices. Harvard family research project has studied how decisions are made and what outcomes are produced. The model above shows information using the normal pathways that were created to give us data. We receive outside information through our sensory gates: the eyes, ears, and mouth. These pathways send messages to the brain, which will retrieve the proper "name" with which that data is associated.

For many years, researchers thought that the heart was constantly responding to the data sent by the brain in the form of neural signals. However, in the most recent studies, they have found that the heart actually sends far more signals to the brain than the brain sends to the heart! These heart signals have a significant effect on how the brain functions with a great influence on emotional processing. The studies have shown that the heart exhibits higher cognitive faculties such as attention, perception, memory, and problem solving. In other words, not only does the heart respond to the brain, but also the brain continuously responds to the heart.

These are very significant scientific findings and I am always amazed how the bible confirms the findings of science. The bible states in Proverbs 23:7 and Proverbs 4:23, *"Above all else, guard your heart, for everything you do flows from it and as a man thinketh in his heart so is he."* The *heart has a huge role in your decision- making.*

INPUTS

The inputs shown in the above diagram are vital to understanding what happens with you spiritually, physically, and mentally. As children, we are exposed to all types of data that come in through the input gates. That is how children grow and begin their intellectual development. We continue this pattern into our adulthood. What we eat, watch, and listen to enters the gates and formulates ideas that is stored as data and rides the neural signals from your brain to your heart and back.

Whatever you are exposing yourself to via your sensory gates has a direct impact on the types and quality of decisions you will make. I attended a conference and Dr. Myles Monroe stated that television is nothing more than a medium with which to transmit ideas. That was a very thought provoking and challenging statement, especially in this age of reality shows, sexually explicit series, and shows that go against the moral values that we know our God exemplifies. I am not making this statement in a judgmental manner banning you from movies and television. In my efforts to be fully transparent, and so we can get all the conviction out of the room, I too was an avid "Scandal" watcher. However, after hearing Dr. Myles make that statement, it made me really think about what ideas I was allowing to be inputted into my brain. I mean, just by the context of the name of the show, Scandal, what messages am I being sold in this very entertaining show?

At the risk of challenging you or getting you really mad at me, just for fun let's list the inputs/ideas we are being sold every week:

* Extra marital affairs are acceptable
* Multiple sexual partners are glamorized
* Pre-martial sex is the norm
* There is no integrity or moral boundaries within our government or world
* There are secret societies that are really above the highest level of government, the Commander and Chief
* You really are empowered to solve any problems you may face even if it means going against everything you know to be right... "The fixer"

I'll stop there on "Scandal," but maybe you should look at some of your inputs and see what ideas you are being sold. It's not an easy thing to palate because I know how, in our high-paced, stressful lives, vegging in front of the TV and posting on social media are how we exhale, but it comes at a price. It is not just television that is the culprit. Music, movies, and video games are huge transmitters of ideas and messages.

INPUT ANALYSIS

When we store the information, then new situations and circumstances will retrieve that stored data and everything will be "filtered" through those thoughts and ideas.

Once the input goes into the brain, it is processed through a lot of "filters" that have been developed over your lifetime. We know these filters as our memory. Wikipedia described memory as the process in which information is encoded, stored, and retrieved. Encoding allows information that is from the outside world to reach our senses in the forms of chemical and physical stimuli. This is vitally important because, as explained earlier, there are neurons that deliver information back and forth from the brain to the heart and they are a huge part of our decision-making.

Storage is the second memory stage or process. This entails that we maintain information over periods of time. We tap into this stored information and see what is being inputted through what is stored. For example, my husband loves tinted lenses in his glasses. When I first met him, all his glasses were tinted yellow. No matter where we went and what we saw, he filtered the visual through yellow glasses, so everything appeared yellow. The interesting thing about that is not everything was really yellow. How it was filtered through his lenses determined the brain's "definition" of what he saw.

In a very similar fashion, the ideas that we are being sold through our sensory gates will become stored data. When we store the information, then new situations and circumstances will retrieve that stored data and everything will be "filtered" through those thoughts and ideas. The dangerous part about that is just like not everything was really yellow that my husband saw, you could be filtering information through tainted ideas and this leads to the type of decisions you will be making.

This is why not all inputs create the same outcomes. Over time the stored information plays a huge role in how you will process ideas. If you have five different people watching the same shows, reading the same books, or listening to the same music at a particular time, then you interview them; the interpretation or summary may sound very different. For example, have you ever listened to different movie critics? Some love it, some hate it, and some just give it an average rating. It is filtered differently for everyone.

It is vital that you learn what good inputs are for you and what is something you need to avoid. When my husband and I were going through marriage problems, it was not to my advantage to latch onto ideas of divorce that would promote thoughts of stepping out on my union. These inputs would just cloud and confuse an already messy situation and produce some really bad decisions. If you struggle with low self-esteem, it is not to your advantage to receive inputs that will foster your feeling bad about yourself and your situations. Watching and listening to sexually explicit shows will not be instrumental in helping a person practice abstinence.

The question that should be coming to mind is how do you counter some of the bad storages that were created and exist so you can change some of your filters? The answer can be found in Romans 12:1-3, *"And be not conformed to this world but be ye transformed by the renewing of your mind, that ye may prove what is that good, and acceptable, and perfect, will of God."* Renewing your mind is a process done by something called meditation. Psalms 1:1-3 states, *"Blessed is the man that walketh not in the counsel of the ungodly, nor standeth in the way of sinners, nor sitteth in the seat of the scornful. But his delight is in the law of the Lord; and in his law doth he meditate day and night. And he shall be like a tree planted by the rivers of water, that bringeth forth his fruit in his season; his leaf also shall not wither; and whatsoever he doeth shall prosper."*

Trees that are planted by rivers of water never wither and die because they are always tied to a continued source of what they need to survive. This book was written to help you not just survive but to thrive. You are built to last because you were created to and you were given all the tools needed for survival. If I were to take you to the most remote and isolated parts of the earth and give you the appropriate tools for survival, and then come back in a week, if you use the tools you will survive. This is the same concept. If you apply the tools outlined in the scriptures, you are given the key to your success.

I am convinced that if we can learn to understand and just master our environments and what we allow into our sensory gates, it would lessen a lot of the heartache, bad decisions, and disappointments we inflict on ourselves. Quite frankly this is not just for believers but for anyone. Science just proves biblical principles, but they are principles that are in operation whether you believe in them or not.

OUTCOMES

Outcomes are the results of the input, input analysis, and summations from all of the neural pathways that ultimately formulate what we think or outcomes. Whatever our thought outcomes are propel us into an action. Everything begins in the mind and is produced to action through this process. If you are going to murder someone, it first begins in your mind. If you are going to have an affair, it first begins in your mind. If you are going to become and alcoholic, it first begins in your mind. What we think produces actions and actions produce outcomes. Let's take a look at Chronicles 28:9. It states "And thou, Solomon my son, know thou the God of thy father, and serve him with a perfect heart and with a willing mind: for the Lord searcheth all hearts, and understandeth all the imaginations of the thoughts."

The power and importance of imaginations are often overlooked. The bible shares a story with us exemplifying the magnitude of the results of what we think. There were generations of people who were descendants of Noah and knew very well about the flood. Out of fear that one day the world could be destroyed by water again, they decided that they would build a tower that would reach all the way to heaven, so they would be safe if that ever happened again. They got together and planned and began to build. The story says God looked over heaven and saw what His children were doing and said if we do not stop them – if they stay on one accord – they will do exactly what needs to be accomplished. They imagined it, got in agreement, and were going to succeed. Imaginations are powerful! Your thoughts are powerful! Your thoughts, what you meditate on, build and produce. The question is, what are you thinking and meditating about? Are you allowing this world's problems, past disappointments, and negative stored data to give a summary analysis that produces derogatory outcomes and negative actions?

Make up your mind today that it has to stop. Evaluate your inputs, storages, and summaries. If any of the input information works negatively against your thought process and against a direction that is going to ultimately be what is positive for you, replace them with positive, uplifting, and goal supporting data. This will ultimately change your outcomes and give you results that show you that you are built to last.

CHAPTER 9: THE FEAR, DOUBT, AND SHAME

> *"Fear produces a false perspective and drives a faulty perception."*

ear, doubt, and shame have such devastating and parasitic effects on people's lives, they warranted a chapter all to themselves. These feelings were a direct root placed in the heart of humanity the moment that we as free-will beings chose a different path than the one laid out by God. Recognizing and understanding these negative traits will help you fight past these feelings that will try to hinder you.

Fear has been defined in so many different ways, but I want to just go back to when it is first mentioned in the bible and see what we can learn. Genesis 3:9-10 gives an account of Adam first experiencing fears.

And the Lord God called unto Adam, and said unto him, Where art thou? And he said, I heard thy voice and I was naked; and I hid myself.

If you study the scripture in context to the whole chapter, you will find that Adam and Eve had just broken a command that God had given them and out of their disobedience, it immediately took them from this beautiful life of walking with God and totally depending on Him to throwing them into this tailspin of despair, fear, and confusion.

> Fear produces a false perspective and drives a faulty perception.

Fear is a bi-product of sin and is very present during our life experiences. The very first thing God says to Adam when he sees this "fear" that became present in the Garden is, "Who told thee that thou wast naked?" In other words, God dealt with them on their perspective of their current situation. How Adam saw his situation immediately directly affected the direction of his feelings and emotions. In this case, that would be emotions and feeling of fear. Fear shows up so easily in the perplexing and troubling times in our lives to try to drive and direct the perspective of our situations.

Perspective is everything! Fear produces a false perspective and drives a faulty perception. Remember our definitions of perspective. It applies so well here I am going to reiterate it again.

- Perspective is a particular attitude toward or way of regarding something, a point of view.
- Perception is defined as the organization, identification, and interpretation of sensory information in order to represent and understand the environment.

When we take a closer look at the repercussions of fear, this is what the two definitions come together and exemplify.

Fear produces a particular attitude toward or way of regarding something and drives a faulty organization, identification, and interpretation of sensory information in order to represent and understand the current environment.

When we are going through something, it totally affects the way we see and comprehend our situations. God realized how powerful and immobilizing fear could be in our lives, so He told us in His Word that this "feeling" does not come from Him. He says in I Timothy 1:7 God hath not given us the spirit of fear; but of power, and of love, and of a sound mind.

I will never forget how fear gripped me to the point that I felt paralyzed. I had just left the hospital from sitting with my mom and was trying to encourage her to keep fighting for her life. She somehow knew that she was not going to make it, but I was unwilling to accept it or let her succumb to that thought. She grabbed my hand and the hand of my husband, said some very personal and penetrating words, put her mask back on her face, and said she was going to sleep. On my journey home, I just knew something wasn't right. At 1:00 in the morning, my phone rang and a doctor called to tell me she went into respiratory distress and they had to intubate her for the third and last time. I just froze in my bed. I knew that this was the last time I would hear my mother's voice, that she would reach for my hand, and the last time she would kiss me good night. I felt like someone had just punched me with all their might and knocked the breath right out of me.

My husband was at the gym and my brothers were at home. I knew I needed to call someone, go to the hospital, pray, do something, but all I could do was lie there and remind myself to breathe. Fear can be all consuming, but what I was feeling did not come from God. It was a spirit that wanted to paralyze and freeze me in the feelings of devastation and despair. If I remained there, it would have affected me, my health and well-being, my family, and ultimately my life's journey.

There are some who may feel that this is a bit dramatic, but there are others reading this book who spend their life stuck in the feelings and emotions that troubling times produce. I am not going to lie; it took me until the sun began to rise to even attempt to move. I have never experienced anything like that before. When the sun began to rise, I looked over at my husband, who was also trying to rest after receiving such devastating news, and I heard a still, small voice say it is time for Chapter 2. This translated into something very important for me during a very dark time. It translated that there was something after losing my mom, that there was something after the problems in my marriage. It was something after the fear that was trying to stop my heart; it translated into hope.

> *Fear cannot coexist with faith.*

We cannot allow fear to settle in and set up camp in our lives at difficult times and keep us from moving forward out of our current situations. We must combat fear with its greatest anecdote, which is faith. Fear and faith cannot coexist. Faith is something that exists on the inside and we all possess a small portion. It is like a muscle. When you exercise it, it grows. When you are going through a difficult time, the challenge acts like weights or dumb bells and it begins to build more mass to your once small portion of faith. Your faith begins to grow and before you know it, fear has fled. By sun up, I had mustered up enough faith to swing my legs over the side of the bed, tend to my children, and with a prayer on my lips face head-on one of the most trying experiences of my life. Fear can be persistent though it would be something that I fought for the remaining four days of my mother's life.

DOUBT

If fear is left unchecked, it results in its very close cousin, doubt. Doubt is defined as having no confidence in someone or something. While you're trying to exercise your faith, doubt quickly shows up alongside fear bringing uncertainty and considering things to be questionable or unlikely. All of a sudden, your entire belief system is shaken to the very core.

As we met with doctor after doctor, and I listened as my older brothers tried to sort through the toughest decision of our lives, doubt flooded in and I literally became physically ill. Remember, I told you these things were introduced in the Garden of Eden. When Adam told God he was naked, he was expressing the state he currently found himself in in that traumatic moment. In reality, he had always been naked, but first fear came and influenced his perception of his situation and very quickly doubt came on the scene. He no longer had confidence in himself or in his God; he was naked.

That's how I felt. I knew I was an Elder in my church, a preacher, a woman of faith, but in that moment fear set in and doubt followed closely behind and I lost all assurance in myself and my God. I am not sure you understand the power doubt can hold over your life. Someone once said if you do not believe in anything, you will fall for everything. When you doubt someone, anything that person does or says doesn't matter because you do not believe in them. I had a hard time seeing how anything good between God and me could happen after going through such a hellish situation. How could I trust Him? How was I going to move forward? Why was He letting this happen to me?

Doubt cannot coexist with belief.

The anecdote to doubt is belief. Simply by its definition, confidence can only be built by gaining, understanding, and believing in something. Doubt cannot coexist with belief.

The night it was decided that we were going to allow my mother to rest and take her off life support. I remember lying in my bed becoming increasingly distressed and all I could do was cry and scream, "Why, why are you doing this to me? After all I've done for you, how could you allow these things to happen to me?"

Once again that still, small voice rang through all the anguish and all I heard was, "Why not you? When I bring you through this, who else will write the book, who else will teach people about what strength rests on the inside of them, who else is going to tell them they are built to last? Why not you? How many more people will you be able to reach? This is not my perfect will. These things are the works of the enemy, but my promise is that everything the wicked one means for your demise, I will turn around for your good. However, you have to believe and know that I am the God of the mountains and the God of the valleys."

At the time I wrote those words down and I was in the midst of my doubt, I had no idea what that meant. As I went back and read through the many things I wrote during this time, I came across the above statement and heard that still, small voice again say, go to I Kings 20:21-28.

The King of Israel went out and smote [the riders of] the horses and chariots and slew the Syrians with a great slaughter. The prophet came to the King of Israel and said to him, Go, fortify yourself and become strong and give attention to what you must do, for at the first of next year the king of Syria will return against you. And the servants of the king of Syria said to him, Israel's gods are gods of the hills; therefore they were stronger than we. But let us fight against them in the plain, and surely we shall be stronger than they. And do this thing: Remove the kings, each from his place, and put governors in their stead. And muster yourself an army like the army you have lost, horse for horse and chariot for chariot. And we will fight against them in the plain, and surely we shall be stronger than they. And he heeded their speech and did so. And at the return of the year, Benhadad mustered the Syrians and went up to Aphek to fight against Israel. The Israelites were counted and, all present, went against them. The Israelites encamped before the enemy like two little flocks of lost kids [absolutely everything against them but Almighty God], but the Syrians filled the country. A man of God came and said to the King of Israel, Thus says the Lord: Because the Syrians have said, The Lord is God of the hills but He is not God of the valleys, therefore I will deliver all this great multitude into your hands, and you shall know and recognize by experience that I am the Lord.

I quickly began to understand two very important things. One, there was a very real enemy that was after me and had every intention of destroying me and two, there was a very real God that had every intention of delivering me out of my trouble and when He did I would know by experience that He is God.

I know this may be difficult for some to understand, so allow me to elaborate more on the story to give you a better understanding as it was so gently explained to me. The enemy will produce bad things in your life. It is his own personal mission statements to kill, steal, and destroy the apples of God's eye, which are you and I. Just like in the story, the enemy went after Israel. Even when Israel won the battle, the enemy would not let it go. He came back thinking the only reason Israel won was because their God was the God of the mountain. That our God only shows up during good times and when things are running well.

The opposing army quickly changed their strategy and brought the best fighters and their best plan striking fear in the heart of Israel and as we have learned doubt quickly followed. It says they were encamped before the enemy like two little flocks of lost kids. In other words, everything was against them. My life and probably areas in your life parallel this passage in the bible. In my situation I quickly realized everything was against me. My marriage was struggling, my mom was gone, and my whole life was hanging on by a string.

The biblical account shares God's perspective when He sees doubt creep in during insurmountable odds. God spoke and said because they have doubted me, because you have doubted me, I am going to show them and you that I am a God of the mountaintop and the valley. Then you will know by experience who I am in your life. He was counteracting doubt with belief. It is one thing to read something and learn facts about it through someone else's eyes and experience. It is another thing to experience it firsthand. Then it becomes personal.

God wants your experience to be personal. He wants you to know firsthand that He is a God that loves you and looks after you turning your doubt to belief. He wanted even me to experience Him in a new way and quickly wanted to change any doubt that I had of Him to true, honest belief.

SHAME

Once doubt shows up on the scene, it challenges everything you believe in and it attacks the very core of what you think about you. After Adam and Eve were afraid and then they doubted, they struggled with shame. This is why they hid themselves. Shame is defined as a painful emotion caused by consciousness of guilt, shortcoming, or impropriety.

Shame is a strong emotion that will keep you from facing your fears, emotions, and situations, so you can begin to build closure and move on with your life. Once my mother had passed away, shame was the final thing to show up. I knew it had arrived because I literally did not want to see anyone. I did not want to go to work, church, or see anyone who knew about what I was going through. I was ashamed. Ashamed is the active, feeling part of shame; it is defined as not wanting *to do* something because of shame or embarrassment. I still could not get past all that had happened to me and I did not want to face people. I did not want to hear "my condolences", "so sorry to hear about your mom", or any of the sentiments that people say in their efforts to make you feel better.

Shame cannot coexist with honor.

I remember going to church and sitting in the back row close to the door, so I could easily slip in and slip out without having to face anyone. After a few weeks of this evasive behavior and being confronted by all the writings that I produced while my mom was in the hospital, I realized I was dealing with that last root of evil, which was shame. The anecdote for shame is honor. I went to a very good girlfriend of mine and told her the enemy was trying to kill me. She gave me these words of wisdom. She stated that it is important, no matter what, to honor myself.

At the time, I thought that was a bizarre statement. Honor is defined as regarding with respect. She went on to explain that I needed to change my perspective. The enemy had taken his best shot and I was still standing. Honor and respect the inner strength that was pushing me forward despite the hellish situation. Although I was hurting and could not see a positive outcome I was still in the fight. You are still in the fight. Honor the God that is in operation in the midst of all of your weaknesses. Shame cannot coexist with honor. It all started to become clearer as I shifted this inner shame with respect and honor. Yes, it appeared that God did not hear my prayers and it felt like I was losing the hardest fight of my life. However, on the other hand, the enemy had taken his best shot and I was still standing, functioning, and taking care of my family. Every day, I was getting out of bed and putting one foot in front of the other. I did not have anything to be ashamed of. It was the exact opposite – the very adversary of my soul had really lost. He could not destroy me. I am built to last and I will choose to shift my focus.

I honor my choice to shift my viewpoint and to survive! I honored myself and most of all, I honored God. I knew it was because of His continued faithfulness to me that He was literally carrying me through a very dark time in my life and for that I was proud not ashamed.

Simply choosing honor to combat the shame empowered me past isolation. What have you been ashamed of and trying to keep hidden and secret? Maybe you are afraid of being judged or looked at differently or people just will not understand. Whatever it is for you, you must understand that your greatest enemy thrives in all of your secrets and while you are in isolation. He works very hard to get you away from your friends, family, your spiritual advisors, and maybe even your church. His greatest advantage is when he can isolate you and make you feel alone and ashamed.

Do not allow this master plan that began all the way in the Garden of Eden to trap you. Fight the temptation to retreat into your own self and work it out alone. It is important to find someone you can trust and open up to them with full transparency. You must be careful whom you choose. Re-read the selection on relationships and select wisely. I believe if you ask God, He will show you with whom to safely share this sensitive information. This will begin your process of turning your shame into honor.

CHAPTER 10: THE NEXT CHAPTER

Our beautiful butterfly, which has survived this horrifying and undoubtedly painful transformation, finds himself changed but wrapped tightly in the chrysalis. It emerges tentatively and, one can only imagine, a bit apprehensively with a totally different image, drive, and purpose than its former state. It no longer has this insatiable desire just to eat but realizes quickly that there are some additions to this new form that are very different. Although the legs and the abdomen seem different but somewhat familiar, there are these wet, deflated, and wrinkled flaps that seem just to hang loosely at its side. It feels the leftover mucous and enzymes that began its transformation resting in his distended abdomen and instinctively begins to pump what's in its abdomen into the veins of its wings to begin to inflate them and give them life.

Much like the beautiful butterfly, you have emerged from your circumstances and situation totally different. What you used to know is at a faint distance with subtle remnants as you study the new you. There is still the strong memory of the pain, heartache, and disappointment that just took place but a glimmer of hope that there is more to the story. At the very periphery of your mind well within reach, there is a hint of possibility. After all you look and feel different and the change had to be for a specific reason. How can something beautiful come from such bad circumstances and experience? You know that transformation has taken place, but what was the objective? What was the purpose and what are you supposed to do now?

PURPOSE

Purpose is defined as the reason something exists or is done, made, or used. It is an all too elusive concept that often finds itself on the back burner of the monotony and business of life. It requires identification, development, and perseverance and it is work.

Purpose lies at the door of everyone's life but is very rarely tapped into due to being inundated with family history, life experiences, and the many obstacles that make it seem almost impossible to reach.

Identification of one's purpose is a self-reflective process that takes time and effort. The majority of people in this world live their entire lives and never grasp hold of what they are passionate about or what drives them to wake up every morning excited about what they are going to accomplish. The key to determining what on earth you are here for starts with two major factors, building mental space and tapping into your purpose.

Building mental space

This world operates at warp speed. Our culture ascribes to the mentality that all things need to be acquired in excess and quickly. It appears that time is fleeting and it is lost so easily. I have noticed that a year goes by almost like a blink of the eye. We cram pack our days with work, sports, church, television and many other activities. Our children may participate in three to four activities a week on top of what we need to do to keep food on the table. It is a rarity that we slow down and even have a chance to think, let alone identify our purpose.

Purpose is well researched and it always fascinates me when its findings line up with the teachings of the bible. Researchers have studied two ways that the mind slows down and de-clutters long enough that it allows for building mental clarity. They suggest that volunteering promotes a mindset that pulls individuals out of their own headspace. Focusing on others, although first perceived as just adding another thing on their plates, seemed to create a significant shift in clarity. It allowed people to think more about their personal lives and how they can be used in a more influential way. The bible addresses this topic when Jesus states that those who give their lives away will find them. In other words, those who are willing to give themselves to others will find their own life and essence – their purpose.

The second study suggests that the moments of surprise or shock have the tendency to shift your focus into the current moment. This jarring can occur when something comes out of nowhere such as a large, unexpected event or tragedy that slows your whole world down.

When it slows, you are presented with something greater than yourself. Purpose is often unearthed and while you are trying to rebound, your perspective, thoughts, and reasoning change and you gain a deeper meaning in your life. The interesting part is that even before the shakeup, there is always a purpose that can often be discovered earlier by looking at the concept of potential.

> *Potential is the pre-cursor to purpose. At the beginning of every purpose-filled life, potential lies dormant waiting to be identified.*

Tapping into your potential:

Let's look at our friend the butterfly. It lies surrounded by the remnants of all it has gone through, totally changed and different than its original state. Although it's wet and uncomfortable, it knows it cannot just stay there. It knows it has to do something to begin to understand and make sense of the new things that are now a part of him. From the moment he emerges from his cocoon and his wings are dry, he can fly, but he won't until he realizes he can fly. The ex-caterpillar must exercise his potential. Potential is the pre-cursor to purpose. At the beginning of every purpose-filled life, potential lies dormant waiting to be identified.

Potential is defined as something that is possible as opposed to actual. This is very important because the majority of the world lives on the edge of what is possible but not realized. The transformed caterpillar has these big, beautiful wings that are lying lifeless by its side. They carry the potential or possibility to give it flight, but if it never taps into that potential it will remain in the current state that it exists. You are born full of untapped potential. God expounds on this idea in Psalms 139:13-16.

> *For you created my inmost being; you knit me together in my mother's womb. I praise you because I am fearfully and wonderfully made; your*

works are wonderful, I know that full well. My frame was not hidden from you when I was made in the secret place, when I was woven together in the depths of the earth. Your eyes saw my unformed body; all the days ordained for me were written in your book before one of them came to be.

The important thing to understand is that no one on this earth was just placed here to exist. There is a very real plan for your life. The scripture says all the days were ordained for you and were written in your book before one of them came to be. God himself saw you being formed in your mother's womb and laid out a plan for your life. That is your potential! It is the original plan that God had for you at conception that is just waiting to be identified.

Identification of your purpose takes action and effort on the part of the one that possesses this inner possibility. When you put forth action and effort, you are beginning to exercise your potential. The transformed caterpillar is an excellent example of these efforts. Once he accepts that he is different and decides that he cannot just lie there and he cannot crawl away like he used to, with almost an instinctive thought, he chooses to use the very thing that initiated this painful change and exercise it to move from a state of potential into a state of purpose. As he pumps the remaining enzymes from his abdomen into his wings, instinctively he recognizes his new addition and catches a glimpse of his purpose being developed.

Truthfully, that is the only reason you are reading these words. With every typed sentence, I was giving my new wings life using the very thing that was meant to destroy me to empower others past their adversity.

We desperately need to follow the example of the transformed caterpillar. When discovering one's purpose, start with what you already know and feel exists. It may begin with the painful experience you are emerging from or have emerged from in the past. It could be a problem that you have recognized that keeps you up at night desiring a solution. Sometimes it is just an innate thing that naturally comes out when you are given an opportunity or placed in the proper environment. Whatever it is for you, it is an opportunity to exercise.

I personally began to exercise my potential when I found myself in the middle of an extremely racially charged atmosphere on my university campus. The president of our university made some unwise public remarks suggesting the African American community lacked the hereditary genetic background to score higher on the SATs. Immediately the campus was divided; the young adults boycotted classes. There was an unbelievable amount of anger and frustration on the campus as a whole. As the president of the Black Student Union, I was immediately placed in the spotlight and became the voice from the African American community on campus. There needed to be a leader and a voice of reason to navigate this political firestorm. With great fear, I began to flap my wings, and with every newspaper article and TV interview I quickly began to exercise the potential of leadership, public speaking, and problem-solving, which constitutes such a huge part of my purpose today.

> *Identification of your purpose takes action and effort on the part of the one that possesses this inner possibility.*

When the tragedies and difficulties you are reading about hit in my personal life, as I emerged different and quite frankly, unsure and shaken, I used what was real and tangible for me at that moment – my pain and disappointment – as fuel to push that potential to another level. With all the feelings and emotions, I knew that if I could muster up the courage to use the excruciating experience, somehow it would help me through the next chapter of my life and to my purpose. Please understand, it does not stop the pain it defines it and gives it purpose. Even more importantly, it would help empower other people to push past the difficulties of life and continue to move forward and overcome great odds and adversity.

DEVELOPMENT

Unfortunately, many people experience growth moments several times in their lives, but growth remains stagnant because they allow the dynamics of the circumstance to steal the power that is just waiting to be developed. An excellent example of this phenomenon is found in Gods very own creation, the arthropods. We can learn so much from these animals as their growth processes are much like ours. Crabs, lobsters and hard shell animals go through several "molting" or growth moments in their lifetimes. Amazingly enough as they are growing, their outer casing becomes too small to accommodate what is growing on the inside of them.

We are so much like this example. As we are going through life's up and downs and transitions, we are faced with the opportunities of evolution. When these moments happen, we have a choice to progress or stay the same. As safe, trusted and cozy as we feel with what was familiar it becomes snug and uncomfortable and if we want something different we must change. The outer familiar casing must shed and a new bigger one must be produced in its place in order to progress. The danger attached to this model is that when you are shedding the old casing that is when you are most vulnerable to the predators in your life. For the arthropods, the time period between the old casing and the new improved outer shell is called the "soft shell" period.

We experience the soft shell period as we are trying to grow in our growth moments. During my transformation time, I was trying to grow my new case that would house my developing purpose. Every time I would resist the urge to give into all of those emotions and feelings, I was one step closer to completing my new bigger covering. The predators of my purpose, sadness, fear, and brokenness continually plagued me and tried to get me to not write this book, teach its principals and produce it in mass so others could overcome. The more I withstood the attacks of the predators I became stronger and stronger.

Development was a conscious choice and decision I was making despite what I was feeling. The definition of development is the act or process of growing or causing something to grow or become larger or more advanced. In my personal situation, I would continually hear a very still, small voice say you are preparing for chapter two. While I was wrestling with sadness, grief, and pain, my mind would vividly re-live the past twenty-nine days of my mom's illness. It was like a skip-ping record, rehearsing the 29 days over and again as if I rehearsed it enough it would have a different outcome. I would plague myself with what if I did this or what if I did that and what could I have done differently. As a believer, I even questioned the power of God in my life why wasn't I anointed enough and how come my prayers did not possess the power to make change. All the complex questions flood in and you ache to gain answers that will just make sense of this change in your life. It was as if even my own subconscious was trying to make sense and gain clarity. However, the only answer it would get, and the only thing that was written in the journal was Gods words, "It is time for Chapter 2".

This happens to so many people in so many different ways. Peo-ple experience job loss, separation and divorce, physical and mental illness, and many life-changing and altering events that thrust them into a new chapter of life. These events create this opportunity of growth and development that transcends their current state.

Unfortunately, many people experience growth moments several times in their lives, but growth remains stagnant because they allow the dynamics of the circumstance to steal the power that is just waiting to be developed. The key to their development of their purpose lies in the choices they are about to make at the moment of impact.

In other words, our butterfly is faced with several options as he lies there not knowing or understanding this new chapter he has begun. He has instinctively launched his potential and sees the new movement in his wings but still has not taken flight. At this pivotal crossroad, he has to make a choice. He can choose to dwell on the memories of being that caterpillar that was quite content just eating and crawling across the leaves. In his new form, he may be having difficulty moving past re-living the excruciating pain that has produced these new wings and cannot see past the pain to test out what the pain produced. Last, he may be allowing the confusion and fear in the moment of lost iden-tity to render himself motionless, and he will let day after day go by as if the transformation never happened. He cannot go back, but he is too afraid to go forward.

> *The scientist in me must caution you that matter is constantly moving. Where there is a lack of movement toward moving forward, the only other option is movement backward.*

There are many butterflies that never take flight. Everything they need is present, but it is not guaranteed that they will fly. This is a lesson for the next chapters in our lives. Our choices, mindsets, and perceptions will drive whether we develop or die. I know die may seem melodramatic; however, the scientist in me must caution you that matter is constantly moving. Where there is a lack of movement toward moving forward, then the only other option is movement backward. Movement is important in our natural bodies. If you just lie down all the time and have a sedentary life, it results in all types of sickness and disease in your body. People who are confined to bed need people to move them or their skin begins to break down and bedsores develop that produce infections, which can lead to death. Movement is vital!

You must choose wisely how you will develop this new purpose, navigate this new chapter, and manage the movement of the emotion, pain, and memory you are experiencing. When all these things work together, much like the muscles, skeletons, and organs in our natural bodies, you will begin to develop a healthy, growing purpose.

PERSEVERANCE

The challenge of growing impatience in our society drastically affects discovering our purpose because it hinders perseverance.

Change is hard and it takes time to grow comfortable in your newly discovered purpose and identity. Time is a process. The challenge we face with the process of time is our current culture and our society does not naturally support this course of action. We have been labeled the "microwave generation" because instant comfort and satisfaction drive our feelings, emotions, and responses to day-to-day activities. For example, where once we would persevere with the process of preparing and cooking a meal when we were hungry, we now tap our fingers standing at the microwave for two minutes and ask what is taking so long.

The process of time to prepare and cook the food with anticipation, resulting in not being hungry, would naturally develop patience because there were no other options to achieve a satisfied, full tummy – at least not until the microwave was created. The new invention shortened a lengthy process to mere seconds producing an instantaneous gratification to hunger. Therefore, patience was no longer needed or developed because you could have what you wanted without endurance. Fast food restaurants became trillion dollar industries building on this feeling and concept and coining catchy phrases like Burger King's, "You can have it your way" in minutes of sitting through a drive thru.

The art of allowing a long process to take its course while you waited and developed patience quickly has become a dying characteristic. We cannot even drive down the road and calmly wait at a traffic light. If the car in front doesn't move instantaneously the moment the light turns green, it can produce such rage that we lean on our horns and hurl insults at each other instead of giving the other person a moment just to drive.

The challenge of the growing impatience in our society drastically affects discovering our purpose because it hinders perseverance. Perseverance is defined as steadfastness in doing something despite difficulty or delay in achieving success. If we quickly grow impatient with the process and any delays that come our way, it can be very tempting to choose a quicker and maybe even easier solution than sticking through the process. There are so many purposes that are derailed for this very reason. Purpose just does not come quickly and easily enough in this society.

I heard Dr. Myles Monroe speak about purpose once and he asked us where we thought the world's greatest riches were held. Magnificent answers were shouted out such as in the Egyptian tombs, buried in the catacombs of some great nation, or maybe in the oil fields in the Middle East. Sadly, he answered our greatest treasures are found lying in the cemeteries across this nation. People buried with the potential of purpose to cure the common cold, books that will never be written, and music that will never be played.

There are very few that will truly live out their full purpose in this earth and go to their resting place content by fulfilling everything that was inside them. In order to accomplish this, it takes time, patience, and tunnel vision.

TUNNEL VISION

> *Persevering through to your purpose requires being able to see where you need to go and to have the ability to funnel all resources, good and bad, that come your way to benefit and drive the goal of achieving your purpose.*

Tunnels are created to focus resources to some type of place or destination. They are used for electricity, water, steam, people and transportation. Tunnels are used to get from one place to the other. Vision is defined as the faculty or state of being able to see. Persevering through to your purpose requires your being able to see where you need to go and having the ability to funnel all resources, good and bad, that come your way to benefit and drive the goal of getting to your purpose. I call this tunnel vision. When you have the ability to block out all distractions and have a clear pathway to the end results, you are operating with tunnel vision. I am smiling as I write these words because it is so much easier said than done, but it is very possible.

I need to remind you that you have a very real enemy whose entire goal is never to have you operate on this earth the way you were originally intended. This is why I stated all resources, good and bad, must be funneled through the tunnel. Resources are a source or supply from which benefit is produced. Anything you go through can be used as a resource but can also act as a hindrance if not tunneled. When you go through good things, it is easy to look at the benefit and use it as a resource. However, it is not as easy to look at the tragedy, disappointments, and failures that enter our lives as a resource. The amazing thing is that they most certainly have potential to be used if you will allow it. You can take these things and funnel them through the tunnel vision, so it does not allow outside influences to stop or hinder the pursuit to purpose.

As I allowed God to deal with me and shift my perspective, I began to funnel the negative experience toward a positive outcome.

For example, losing my mother and increasing marriage problems had the dangerous potential to cause me to slip into depression. I certainly felt myself fighting every day not to just have a breakdown that would render me immobile. Despite how I felt, I knew that something was very different and I was changing. I knew there was something positive that had to come out of such a terrible experience. As I allowed God to deal with me and shift my perspective, I began to funnel the negative experience toward a positive outcome. I began to think about all the people I could now minister to who suffered a tragic lost. For years, I have dealt with people who were grieving. Grieving lost loved ones, businesses, dreams and marriages. Now, I understood so much better that type of hurt and the pain that goes along with such losses. I moved from just giving lifeless, encouraging words to empathizing from experience. It gave me a different type of influence and validation in that area knowing that I had been through it and came out of it still standing. I was funneling my experience into tunnel vision and it was moving me closer and closer to my purpose.

I am not saying it is easy. Even as I write these words, every day I have to stay focused and not let sadness and grief overwhelm me. However, every day I get stronger and that much closer. You can do the same! You can take things that are meant to destroy you and funnel them through the tunnel vision.

THE CONCLUSION

Becoming built to last is a journey that you have a lifetime to fulfill, but it is only obtained by the persistent and courageous. It is my forty-third birthday as I conclude this book. I am not an accomplished writer and never thought I would author a book. I am not sure what comes next. All I know is I put my feelings, thoughts, and struggles on paper and walked through each chapter live and in color in my very own life. With every keystroke, just hoping and praying that somehow it would snatch a person from despair and build some ground under their feet to fight another day.

I wish I could end this book with a happily ever after ending, but the truth is today I am not "feeling" happy. The pain for me today is as sharp as it was back at Chapter 1. The difference now though is the tears will dry a little quicker and every day it is just a little easier to refocus and move on to whatever is next. It has produced a strange dichotomy of sadness but joy at the same time. Joy is not something that is relegated or bound by "feeling" happy. It is something that comes from God and life's circumstances cannot steal it away.

I am working through my Chapter 2 and that is my testimony at this point in my journey. I am working through it, but I am not alone. My God promised He would never leave me or forsake me and He has shown himself to me personally as a God that comforts, delivers and sets free to fly just like our beautiful butterfly. Every day He brings me comfort and then when I am comforted, I look for opportunities to comfort someone else.

You can do the same thing. While I am still trying to find my way, I am not where I used to be. There have been so many difficulties and hard times, but every rough road has polished my life. I have found my wings and my purpose is unfolding. It has come with a cost and maybe yours does too, but do not give up. Press through the pain. God has a plan!

You are Built to Last.

STUDY WORKBOOK

This workbook was created to assist you in working through some of the details in each chapter. I suggest you read the chapters and go through the workbook simultaneously to assist in creating a thought provoking experience. Adding this resource to reading the book will give you greater insight that will propel you to be Built to Last.

Chapter 1 - The Human

> *Your creator embedded answers to the very thing that worries you, keeps you up at nights and continually makes life very difficult on the inside of you.*

What worries you and keeps you up at night? List here all the things that are a constant weight on you.

_____

_____

_____

_____

_____

_____

_____

_____

Humanistic Realm vs Spiritual Realm:

- **The degree of the attack on your life is indicative of the level of strength that lies on the inside of you.**

- The biggest question that challenges making the switch from the human realm to the spiritual realm is, why me. It is the constant focus on feeling versus the deeper question that only the brave dig to answer and that is why not you.

Describe current situations in your life that you are experiencing difficulty transitioning from the humanistic realm to the spiritual realm.

_____

_____

_____

_____

_____

_____

_____

_____

Living in the spiritual realm allows you to see beyond what is facing you, and go to deeper levels of what God is showing you in the midst of the challenge. Look at the list you made above what could it be that God is trying to show you in the spiritual realm?

_____

_____

_____

_____

_____

_____

_____

_____

_____

Chapter 2 - The Olive

> *Whatever rests on the inside will spill out and be revealed.*

Think carefully about the last time you were in a pressure situation. This could be driving down the road and someone cuts you off, relationship challenges or any personal battle you are fighting. How are you handling yourself during these difficulties? What is coming out of you?

_____

_____

_____

_____

_____

_____

_____

_____

There are so many things deep on the inside of you that have great value and great worth. The bible teaches that it is a treasure in earthen vessels, and that you really are fearfully and wonderfully made, and created on purpose, specifically designed for great purpose. God had you on his mind, and when He began to place the treasure on the inside and wrap it in human flesh, he knew there would a process to get to what was on the inside.

Now that you understand that there is a process to get to the treasure that is in your earthen vessel, from the list above what do you think you need to do differently?

_____

_____

_____

_____

_____

_____

_____

_____

Please remember: What is vitally important is for you to understand what is happening to you, and humbly with courage, push through the pain. Just when the olive looks annihilated, a separation begins to form. The outside casing – the fleshy part of who you are – divides, and a beautiful, pure portion of you emerges from the destruction. Slowly, the very thing that was meant to destroy you, in a miraculous way, turns into something that has made you better, more effective, and much more valuable. Mary is crushed beyond recognition and lying before Jesus, hopeless. Just when everyone in that room counted her out, Jesus begins to speak and teach all that are watching that not only is she forgiven, but also her life-changing act of humility will ensure that she will never be the same. Her healing, peace, her call, her purpose, her destiny and prosperity came from going through a painful process of dying to herself. When you are being crushed beyond recognition, there is something miraculous happening deep on the inside.

God knew what was going to happen to Mary. He knew what was going to happen to me, and He knows what is going to happen to you.

Chapter 3 - The Oil

> *God made sure that the very thing that was created to destroy you would produce such greatness on the inside of you; it would destroy the enemy's kingdom.*

This chapter outlines a very important parable about the five wise and five foolish virgins. The foolish virgins had everything they needed to meet the bridegroom, but because they didn't go the extra step and pay the price for the extra oil, they missed out on the very thing they were headed out to do – to meet the bridegroom; they missed out on being with Jesus. The wise virgins had chosen to pay the price to carry the extra oil. It was probably inconvenient and they probably didn't feel like carrying the extra oil with them, but they were willing to pay the price and endure the extra burden so that no matter what, they wouldn't miss Jesus.

Reflect on how this may apply in your life. List any areas of your life that you are living on the convenience basis versus the purposed goal driven choice. Are there areas of your life that you know God is asking you to sacrifice? You know he is asking you to do something, change a behavior or go after a vision. Despite knowing, you have not found the time, gathered the boldness and the courage or not made what God is saying to you a priority.

_____

_____

_____

_____

_____

_____

Now that you have identified these areas, list three steps that you can take ___for each___ to make a change. Remember, the anointing is very special, and it is something that God desires all of His children to possess. It is very sad to say that not everyone will experience this power in and on their lives. It is a privilege to allow God to operate in you and flow out of you in a way that impacts not only your life, but also the lives of anyone that is around you.

_____

_____

_____

_____

_____

_____

_____

_____

Chapter 4 - The Transformation

Everything transforms into something purposed.

No matter how hard that caterpillar may have fought to keep crawling and eating there was something propelling it to achieve the greatness on the inside. It could not control the drive to eat the last leaf, climb the tree and begin to wrap a cocoon around him. It was going to become a butterfly. The principal is the same for you. God placed something "special" on the inside of you that will always push you forward to the greatness and purpose on the inside of you. When your discomfort comes, no matter how hard, it creates something new on the inside of you that takes shape and grows. You were not created to stay the same: you were created to transform! Transformation often happens during difficult times or as addressed in our reading in the valley.

God wants us to identify in the valley. Yes, it is a horrible, hurtful place that is trying to develop and mold a lasting impression in our lives. In some situations, it hurts so badly that it leaves us catatonic and immobile. It takes every ounce of energy to just swing our legs over the side of the bed in order to handle the mandatories in our lives. While we are in the midst of all of that, and while I am experiencing all of this in the midst of typing, God wants us to see beyond what we are seeing, feeling, and experiencing. This can only be accomplished by identifying something bigger than the challenge we are facing. You must, and I must, pinpoint the mountain in the midst of the valley and view it from that higher point of view.

Review the transformation chapter again and really think about the valley areas of your life and write them below. When you identify them list next to them the mountaintop that rest in that valley. Create quiet time and ask God what does he want you to see from a higher point of view. List what you hear below.

_____

_____

_____

_____

_____

_____

_____

_____

Chapter 5 - The Parasitoids

Parasitoids are parasitic insects that live on a single host with one goal in mind. It lives to reproduce itself on the inside of something or someone and the parasitoid larvae spend their time eating their host from the inside out. They literally suck the very life out of you in a selfish, self-serving manner until it is finished with you. Relationships, patterns of behavior decisions, fear, doubt and shame are huge destructive forces in our lives.

Chapter 6 - Relationships

> *Wayward relationships are used to snuff out a lot of the purpose that is supposed to exist on this earth.*

On a separate sheet of paper, list all of the influential relationships that you have in your life. Next to each name list the positives and the negatives that have developed out of the association. For the ones that their negative contributions outweigh their positive list below as an identified parasitoid in your life:

_____

_____

_____

_____

_____

_____

_____

_____

_____

_____

_____

Chapter 7 - Patterns of Behavior

> *At the core of every action, there is something that is initiating the thought that drives that action.*

Knowing yourself is a powerful tool that is not often tapped into, which helps individuals to introspect and gives them a different viewpoint regarding how information is being processed. Although to some, this may seem like a very obvious observation, there are so many who go through life and never really know themselves. It is very easy to go through life making decisions, working on jobs, raising families and just dealing with the day to day of life and never take the time to find out who you really are and what drives all of those actions.

Consider for a moment your past behaviors. This is not a time to make excuses no one is here right now in this moment but you and God. What are some disappointing things that you have done and allowed to take place in your life? It is important you do not justify during this exercise. There are many that have been doing certain destructive things for so long that the enemy has tricked you into thinking your patterns of behavior are justified. A way to identify the truth is to match it against the Word of God. Please list below some of the disturbing behaviors.

_____

_____

_____

_____

_____

_____

_____

> *Every behavior yields a result and produces some-thing that can replicate over and over again for generations to come.*

   Take a moment to think about your family and the generations before you. If you do not know anything about your family, go to your family and begin to ask questions. I know this may seem tedious, but the bible teaches us to know the enemy's devices. Past generation mistakes could be passing down to you and you need to be the generation that makes the change. List what you find out below (i.e. divorce, poverty, selfishness, anger). Do you see any similarities that you are currently repeating? List them below.

_____

_____

_____

_____

_____

_____

_____

_____

> *Your weakness is not your weakness. It is your failure to identify and then deal with that weakness that is your true frailty.*

For those that are really ready to destroy the parasitoid of negative patterns of behavior, it would greatly benefit you to go to two or three people that love you. I mean that truly love you and have supported you in the good and the bad. Ask and liberate them to give you a list of the weaknesses they have seen in your life. List them below:

_____

_____

_____

_____

_____

_____

_____

Now that you have listed the areas that you need to work on generationally and individually, review what you read on new wine skins. What must you do to make change and produce the new wine skins in your life?

_____

_____

_____

_____

_____

_____

_____

_____

_____

_____

_____

_____

_____

_____

_____

_____

_____

_____

_____

_____

Chapter 8 - Decisions, Decisions, Decisions

> *Well thought out choices of today are the driving force for tomorrow's well executed results, and position us well for the next day's choices; Poor, rash, and impulsive choices of today lead to many devastating ripple effects of results that can be felt for generations.*

After reviewing the outcome based decision model, list the negative inputs that are daily affecting your decision-making? It is important to prayerfully consider this list because there maybe some things you mindlessly listen to, watch or entertain not immediately realizing its impact. Refer to my example of the show Scandal.

_____

_____

_____

_____

_____

_____

_____

Now that you have listed those inputs, what positive inputs will you exchange in the place of the negative inputs to change the outcomes in your life.

_____

_____

_____

_____

_____

_____

_____

Remember: I am convinced that if we can learn to understand and master our environments it will be life changing. When we closely monitor what we allow into our sensory gates, it would lessen a lot of the heartache, bad decisions, and disappointments we inflict on ourselves. Quite frankly this is not just for believers but for anyone. Science just proves biblical principles, but they are principles that are in operation no matter what you believe.

Chapter 9 - Fear, Doubt and Shame

Fear, doubt, and shame have such devastating and parasitic effects on people. They can be so life altering they warranted a chapter all to themselves. These feelings and emotions were a direct root placed in the heart of humanity the moment that we as free-will beings chose a different path than the one laid out by God. Recognizing and understanding these negative traits will help you fight past these feelings that will try to hinder you.

Fear

Fear is a bi-product of sin and is very present during our life experiences. The very first thing God says to Adam when he sees this "fear" that became present in the Garden is, "Who told thee that thou wast naked?" In other words, God dealt with them on their perspective of their current situation. How Adam saw his situation immediately directly affected the direction of his feelings and emotions. In this case, that would be emotions and the feeling of fear. Fear shows up so easily in the perplexing and troubling times in our lives to try to drive and direct the perspective of our situations.

Review the definitions of perspective and perception. Now that you understand how fear affects perspective and drives perception. List some things that you know are causing fear in your life. (i.e. For me, it is the completion of this book and stepping into another level of helping people). What is it for you?

_____

_____

_____

_____

_____

_____

_____

Since we learned that fear cannot coexist with faith, what do we need to resolve to trust right now? Take the fears above and list the faith statement that will counteract the fear. **For my fear: I trust God for the strength, courage and boldness to complete this book and that it will be used to help people navigate all the different areas of their lives, discover their purpose and live victoriously while doing great damage to the enemies kingdom.** List below your faith statements and then place on 3x5 cards to post where you can review them on the daily basis:

_____

_____

_____

_____

_____

_____

Doubt

If fear is left unchecked, it results in its very close cousin, doubt. Doubt is defined as having no confidence in someone or something. While you're trying to exercise your faith, doubt quickly shows up alongside fear bringing uncertainty and considering things to be questionable or unlikely. All of a sudden, your entire belief system is shaken to the very core.

Doubt cannot coexist with belief. When you believe something you do not doubt. List the things that you do not believe God for anymore. Be honest. He already knows.

_____

_____

_____

_____

_____

Then take the list one step further and read **Mark 9:20-24**: Consider this father who is desperate for his son to be healed. He goes to Jesus and although he wanted change for his son so bad, he realized that the change was contingent on belief. He could not doubt. In first recognizing that he had doubt, he asked Jesus to help his unbelief. Sit quietly before God and ask God in this moment to replace your doubt with belief.

Shame

Once doubt shows up on the scene, it challenges everything you believe in and it attacks the very core of what you think about you. After Adam and Eve were afraid and then they doubted, they struggled with shame. This is why they hid themselves. Shame is defined as a painful emotion caused by consciousness of guilt, shortcoming, or impropriety.

List some of the guilt and shortcomings you are wrestling.

_____

_____

_____

_____

_____

_____

Shame cannot coexist with honor. **Remember:** honor is regarding with respect. In order to combat the shame you have to muster up enough respect for you and for your God. The evidence that you are reading this proves that it is not over yet. You are reading, walking, talking and reasoning that means there is an opportunity for change. Begin with that small thought. He has taken his best shot and you are still breathing. As you nurture that small seed of honor, build on it. List the things that despite the enemy's best shot you are doing or have been able to do?

_____

_____

_____

_____

_____

_____

_____

Start with honoring these things even though you may feel they are insignificant. Honor the small steps and honor the God of the small steps. The bible teaches us to not despise small beginnings. If you continue to do this, shame will have to go because shame and honor cannot coexist.

Chapter 10 - The Next Chapter

The next chapters of your life and my life are all about purpose. Purpose is defined as the reason something exists or is done, made, or used. It is an all too elusive concept that often finds itself on the back burner of the monotony and business of life. It requires identification, development, and perseverance; it is work.

After reading on mental space, list the areas in your life that are cluttered and keep you from clearly functioning and identifying purpose in your life.

_____

_____

_____

_____

_____

_____

_____

Consider some of the suggested ways to clear some mental space. What are some action steps to unclutter the things listed above?

_____

_____

_____

_____

_____

_____

_____

Once you have established some clarity, list some of the identified potential that needs to be realized and developed in your life. What are some of the things that you know you do well? What produces positive outcomes in your life and others confirm those outcomes?

Side note: Even if you are like me and have difficulty in seeing and accepting those things, put them on your list. This may be a targeted area of growth that you need to truly honor and allow God to grow.

_____

_____

_____

_____

_____

_____

_____

Once you have identified the potential what actions steps can you take to develop the potential?

_____

_____

_____

_____

> *Perseverance is defined as steadfastness in doing something despite difficulty or delay in achieving success.*

There are far too many of us that quit to soon. Persevering through to your purpose requires being able to see where you need to go and to have the ability to funnel all resources, good and bad, that come your way to benefit and drive the goal of achieving your purpose.

After reading about tunnel vision, what do you need to do to produce tunnel vision?

_____

_____

_____

_____

_____

_____

_____

This workbook was created to be a continual resource. A lot that is listed on this page needs to be reviewed over and over again as your life evolves and changes. As you continue to grow and mature, new challenges develop that need to be addressed. Life is a cyclical pattern of continued growth. Use this workbook over and over again to evaluate and re-evaluate the unique God given choice and ability that he has given you to be **Built to Last!**

For book information contact:
Phone: 856-318-9479
Email: majmichelljohnston@gmail.com